SECTION 1:
INTRODUCTION – HOW THIS BOOK WILL HELP YOU

Parenting can be the most rewarding job on earth—and sometimes the toughest. You cradle your newborn the first time and promise, either silently or aloud, to provide the best life possible for him or her. The years quickly fly by—and suddenly, your youngster is about to enter school.

If you're like most people, that is a scary day. *How will little Sara react to being away from me? What will happen if Noah misbehaves? Will the teacher provide the attention that Riley needs in order to learn?*

As your child grows older and continues to achieve new milestones, your concerns grow, too. *Can I trust Sara being home alone after school until I get home? What will Noah do if his friends offer him a cigarette? Will Riley's friends tempt her to try drugs?*

These types of worries are normal and show that you are a loving, attentive parent who wants what is best for your child. Reading this booklet also shows that you are concerned and that you want to help your child achieve a healthy, drug-free lifestyle from preschool through high school—a dozen or so critical years when attitudes about drug use are formed. Many school districts across the country have had to cut funding for alcohol and drug education programs, making it even more important that you are informed, consistent, and current when you communicate with your child about drugs and alcohol.

DID YOU KNOW ...

According to a national survey called Monitoring the Future (MTF) taken in 2011[1]

› Daily marijuana use is now at a 30-year peak level among high school seniors. One in every 15 high school seniors today is smoking pot on a daily or near daily basis.

› Energy drinks are being consumed by about one-third of teens, with use highest among younger teens. These drinks are particularly dangerous—even deadly—when consumed with alcohol.

› Although rates of smoking have declined among youths, 40 percent have tried cigarettes by 12th grade, and 10 percent of 12th graders are daily smokers.

› Alcohol remains the most widely used drug by today's teenagers. Despite recent declining rates, seven out of every 10 students have consumed alcohol (more than just a few sips) by the end of high school, and one-third of students have done so by the eighth grade.

› One of every nine high school seniors said they've used synthetic marijuana, sometimes called K2/Spice, within the previous 12 months.

HOW TO USE THIS BOOKLET

Rather than reading this publication from front to back as you would read a book, we hope you will use the Table of Contents to find a topic that interests you or to find a specific substance you'd like to know more about. We've also included some personal stories from parents who've lost children to drugs and a Resource section in the back that suggests online sources where you or your children can learn more.

> The proportion of 12th-graders misusing psychotherapeutic prescription drugs (i.e., amphetamines, sedatives, tranquilizers, or narcotics other than heroin) is over 15 percent.

This publication was designed to help you understand

> The substances children are exposed to and where they get them. It will explain the names (and "street names") of common drugs, how they're used, their effects, where children obtain them, and how to know if your child is using them.

> Which children are most at risk for using drugs and how you can offset some of those *risk factors*.

> The importance of providing what are called *protective factors*—at home, in school, and in the community.

> How to talk to your children about drugs and alcohol. It will suggest ways to initiate conversations with your child at different ages and at various stages of physical and mental development.

> What role social media play in what your child learns about drugs.

> The steps to take if you suspect your child may already be using drugs or alcohol.

This booklet also provides answers to questions your child may have and resources you can use to find more information or get help with your concerns. It covers important topics such as

> Why drinking alcohol—**even once**—is a serious matter. Each year, approximately 5,000 young people under the age of 21 die as a result of underage drinking, which is more than from all illegal drugs combined.[2]

> The importance of maintaining a close relationship with your child. A child who gets through age 21 without smoking, using illegal drugs, or abusing alcohol is much less likely to do so as an adult.[3] No one has greater power to influence your child's behavior than **YOU** do, and a close bond can spare your child the negative experiences associated with illegal drug use. It may even save your child's life.

Throughout this publication, we refer to what you, as a *parent*, can do. However, raising a drug-free child is seldom done alone. Children also spend time with other caregivers—older siblings, aunts and uncles, family friends, stepparents, grandparents, extended family members, and many others who have the power to influence them. So when we say "parents" on these pages, we really mean all of the caregivers in your child's life. We also encourage you to share the information here with them so that your child receives consistent information.

We hope this booklet answers many of the questions you have about raising a drug-free child. For more information, please also visit the following websites.

> United States Drug Enforcement Administration: **www.justice.gov/dea**

> Get Smart About Drugs: **www.getsmartaboutdrugs.com**

> National Institute on Drug Abuse: **www.nida.nih.gov**

> The Partnership at Drugfree.org: **www.drugfree.org**

> National Institute on Alcohol Abuse and Alcoholism: **www.niaaa.nih.gov**

Additional resources are listed at the back of this publication.

WHAT DO YOU BELIEVE?

A *myth* is something we believe without having any proof one way or the other. Many parents maintain myths about drugs because it is easier than finding out or accepting the truth.

Believing a myth doesn't make it true, just like denying that a problem exists does not mean there isn't one. And if trouble signs appear, ignoring them won't make the problem go away.

MYTH #1: MY CHILD ISN'T EXPOSED TO DRUGS AND WOULDN'T DO THEM ANYWAY

Some parents don't believe their child has access to drugs and alcohol, or they think, "My child would never do anything so risky." These are serious misconceptions!

Sadly, children of all ages are exposed to drugs. In 2011, almost 26 percent of youths had been offered, sold, or given an illegal drug on school property, according to a national survey of ninth-through 12th-grade students in public and private schools.[4] Children being in this type of environment is alarming, since the earlier a child begins to smoke, drink, or use drugs, the likelier that child is to become addicted.

Additionally, CASA's 2011 National Survey of American Attitudes on Substance Abuse[5] found that almost one in four middle school students perceive their school as *drug-infected* (meaning drugs are used, kept, or sold on school grounds); the number jumps to more than 60 percent for high school students.[6] Compared to teens attending drug-free schools, teens attending drug-infected schools are

› Twice as likely to have used tobacco, alcohol, and marijuana

› Almost twice as likely to be able to get alcohol in an hour or less

FAMILY TIES

The National Center on Addiction and Substance Abuse (CASA) defines *family ties* as the quality of the relationship between teens and their parents, how often parents argue with one another, how good teens say their parents are at listening to them, how often teens attend religious services, and how often the family has dinner together. In a National Survey of American Attitudes on Substance Abuse,[7] CASA researchers learned that compared to teens in families with strong family ties, teens in families with weak family ties are

• Four times likelier to have tried tobacco

• Four times likelier to have tried marijuana

• Almost three times likelier to have tried alcohol

› Two-and-a-half times as likely to be able to get marijuana in an hour or less

› One-and-a-half times as likely to be able to get prescription drugs without a prescription in an hour or less

So it is **NOT** a myth that drugs are available. The question is whether **YOUR** child is getting them—and using them.

› One in four kids who have tried alcohol had their first drink at age 12 or younger.[8]

› Every day, more than 4,000 teens try an illicit drug for the first time.[9]

› Some 60 percent of teens who have abused prescription painkillers to get high did so before age 15.[10]

› By the time they graduate high school, about 44 percent of U.S. teens will have tried marijuana at least once.[11]

MYTH #2: IT'S NORMAL FOR KIDS TO EXPERIMENT WITH DRUGS

Some parents believe that experimenting with drugs or alcohol is a normal part of growing up. Those parents are wrong. Alcohol poisoning can occur when someone drinks enough alcohol to depress the nerves that control

involuntary actions such as breathing and the gag reflex (which prevents choking). A fatal dose of alcohol caused by alcohol poisoning can happen the very first time a child drinks alcohol, causing serious brain damage or death.

Also, it's extremely dangerous to minimize the effects of one substance compared to another. The 2011 CASA survey revealed that teens who have used tobacco are 11 times likelier to have used marijuana than teens who have never used tobacco. And simply trying marijuana one time can lead your child to experiment with other drugs and put them at risk for abuse.

Experimenting with drugs or alcohol is not normal. **USE** can lead to **ABUSE**, which can lead to **ADDICTION**, so *any* use is unacceptable.

MYTH #3: I CAN'T CHANGE MY CHILD'S FUTURE

While it's true that children often idolize sports heroes and celebrities, they also idolize **YOU**. As a parent or caregiver, you have the power to help shape their attitudes about drugs. One way to do that is by talking to them regularly about what is going on in their lives. Kids who learn a lot about the risks of drugs and alcohol from their parents are up to 50 percent less likely to use than those who do not.[12]

Talking to your child about drugs and alcohol doesn't mean lecturing. In fact, there are many things you can do (or may already do!) to provide the type of environment that may keep your child from experimenting with drugs or alcohol.

Talking to your child about drugs and alcohol doesn't mean lecturing. In fact, there are many things you can do (or may already do!) to provide the type of environment that may keep your child from experimenting with drugs or alcohol. One is to spend more time with your child. A 2011 national survey about the importance of family dinners revealed that 18 percent of teens said they would like to spend more time with their parents.[13] That's important because those who spent seven hours or less per week with their parents were twice as likely to have used alcohol and twice as likely to have tried drugs (including marijuana and prescription drugs) to get high. Imagine! Simply spending time with your children may make them less likely to try drugs or alcohol!

Family dinners are an excellent way to spend time with your child. And make no mistake—those family dinners matter. Teens who have fewer than three family dinners per week are almost four times as likely to have used tobacco, more than twice as likely to have used alcohol, and two-and-a-half times as likely to have used marijuana. Family dinners don't have to be elaborate or expensive. Think of simple, inexpensive ways to make the

meal fun, such as eating a picnic meal in the back yard, having a contest to see who can create the best pizza, or setting up a burger bar with outrageous toppings. Enjoy the process, and spend the time together talking with your children about their day.

Simply being there for your child—day or night—is also helpful. A child who feels you are available will be more likely to come to you with questions about drugs or challenges with peer pressure or other situations that make your child feel uncomfortable. It is especially important to be there for your child during times of transition, such as changing schools, moving, or divorce, because the risk of drug use increases greatly during these times.[14] As children advance from elementary school to middle school, for example, they face new social situations. They will be exposed to cigarettes and alcohol—if they haven't been already—and friends may encourage them to try new things. As they later go from middle school to high school, they will face a larger variety of substances and have more of a desire to fit in or seem cool to their classmates.

Additionally, teens who attend religious services four or more times a month are less likely to have used tobacco (11 percent vs. 3 percent), consumed alcohol (27 percent vs. 13 percent), or used marijuana (15 percent vs. 5 percent) than those who attend such services less frequently or not at all.[15]

Remember, preventing the first use prevents abuse, and preventing abuse prevents addiction. You **can** change your child's future.

MYTH #4: MY KIDS DON'T CARE WHAT I THINK

Kids—especially teenagers—sometimes act like they don't care what their parents think. Studies have shown, however, that they *do* care.

According to a 2010 national survey by the Substance Abuse and Mental Health Services Administration (SAMHSA), youths aged 12 to 17 were less likely to use a substance if they believed their parents would strongly disapprove.[16] This was particularly true for tobacco and marijuana.

Your children *do* listen to you, even if they roll their eyes and pretend not to. Don't want them drinking or using drugs? Tell them how you feel and what you expect from them. For example, you might say

> "I want you to have fun and enjoy this time in your life, but I also want you to stay healthy because I love you. The best way to do that is to stay completely away from drugs and alcohol. Can you promise me that you will?"

> "I know you may be tempted to try drugs, but I also know you're really smart. That's why I expect you to stay clean—no matter what your friends do. Agreed?"

> "It scares me to know how easily you could damage your brain or get addicted to something. Will you give me your word that you won't try things just because the people you hang out with try them?"

Your children **do** care what you say, but you have to tell them what you think—and what you expect.

MYTH #5: IT'S OKAY FOR ME TO USE BECAUSE I'M AN ADULT

Some parents may believe that because they are adults, it's okay for them to drink alcohol excessively or to smoke cigarettes (even marijuana) even though they tell their children not to do it. This is especially true if adults think their use isn't affecting their family. But because your children look up to you, they want to *be* like you.

So when they see you smoking, they are going to think it is okay for them to do it, too, no matter what you say. However, if they watch as you struggle to quit smoking, they understand the difficulty of breaking the addiction.

Similarly, if you come home from work complaining that you had a hard day and drink heavily and excessively, or drive while under the influence of alcohol, you may be sending an unintended message. It is certainly not a message about drinking responsibly.

Some parents choose to believe this myth because they are in denial about their *own* behavior and don't like to think about how their own drug or alcohol use is affecting their children. One in four children in the United States is exposed to alcoholism or drug addiction in the family,[17] and these kids have a significantly increased risk of becoming alcoholics themselves when they grow up.

So if you portray your beliefs about the danger of using drugs and alcohol through your actions, your child is more inclined to believe you. And if you have a problem with tobacco, alcohol, or drugs, speak to your family doctor about getting help.

MYTH #6: I DON'T WANT TO ALIENATE MY CHILD BY BEING TOO STRICT

In some homes today, parents try very hard to be a friend to their child, and this interferes with their ability to be an effective parent. Consequently, some parents are afraid to set rules and enforce them.

But children *need* a clear understanding of your expectations. Sure, they may test you occasionally by pushing the boundaries of the rules you set. But that is the exact moment when you must be a parent—an enforcer—and follow through with whatever consequences you outlined as punishment.

Developing a strong bond with your child at an early age is important, but it needs to be a parent-child bond in which **YOU** take control. The best way to do that is to (1) set rules and (2) enforce them consistently.

1   Johnston, L. D., O'Malley, P. M., Bachman, J. G., and Schulenberg, J. E. *Monitoring the Future national results on adolescent drug use: Overview of key findings*, 2011. National Institute on Drug Abuse. Ann Arbor: Institute for Social Research, The University of Michigan. 2012.

2   National Institutes of Health. National Institute on Alcohol Abuse and Alcoholism. *Underage Drinking*. Alcohol Alert, Publication Number 67. January 2006.

3   The National Center on Addiction and Substance Abuse (CASA) at Columbia University. *National Survey of American Attitudes on Substance Abuse XVI: Teens and Parents*. August 2011.

4   Centers for Disease Control and Prevention. *Trends in the Prevalence of Tobacco, Alcohol, and Illegal Drug Use on School Property. National Youth Risk Behavior Survey 1991–2011*. Accessed September 21, 2012, **www.cdc.gov/healthyyouth/yrbs/pdf/us_taodu_trend_yrbs.pdf**.

5   *National Survey of American Attitudes on Substance Abuse XVI: Teens and Parents*.

6   Ibid.

7   The National Center on Addiction and Substance Abuse (CASA) at Columbia University. *National Survey of American Attitudes on Substance Abuse XV: Teens and Parents*. August 2010.

8   The Police and Communities Together (PACT 360) website. Home page, accessed September 21, 2012, **http://pact360.org/programs/parents360**.

9   Ibid.

10 The Partnership at DrugFree.org website. Home page, accessed September 21, 2012, **http://notinmyhouse.drugfree.org**.

11 U.S. Department of Health and Human Services, National Institutes of Health. *Marijuana: Facts Parents Need to Know. A Letter to Parents*. NIH Publication No. 10-4036. Printed 1995, Revised November 1998, November 2002, September 2004, August 2007, March 2011. Reprinted April 2001, February 2007.

12 The Partnership at DrugFree.org sponsored website. Home page, accessed September 21, 2012, **www.drugfree.org/prevent**.

13 The National Center on Addiction and Substance Abuse (CASA) at Columbia University. *National Survey of American Attitudes on Substance Abuse XV: Teens and Parents*. September 2011.

14 National Institute on Drug Abuse. *Drugs, Brains, and Behavior - The Science of Addiction*. NIH Pub No. 10-5605. Printed April 2007. Revised February 2008, August 2010.

15 *National Survey of American Attitudes on Substance Abuse XVI: Teens and Parents*.

16 Substance Abuse and Mental Health Services Administration. Center for Behavioral Health Statistics and Quality. *Results from the 2010 National Survey on Drug Use and Health: Summary of National Findings*. NSDUH Series H-41, HHS Publication No. (SMA) 11-4658. September 2011.

17 Tian Dayton, PhD. *Portrait of an Alcoholic Family: Forgotten Children; Right Next Door?* National Association for Children of Alcoholics. Kensington, MD. (n.d.) Accessed September 21, 2012, **www.nacoa.org/pdfs/Portrait%20of%20an%20Alcoholic%20Family.docx.pdf**.

NOTE: Please also see the **Drug Identification Chart** at the end of this publication.

Children today are exposed to drugs and alcohol because they see them used in movies, in music videos, and on television from a very young age. They also learn about them on social networking sites, where information is instant and available 24/7, and they learn from classmates. Exactly *what* they learn depends on what they listen to, read, or watch, and who they hang out with.

At the end of this publication is a detailed **Drug Identification Chart** that lists many drugs commonly abused today, along with the side effects and "street names." In this section, we'll talk about some commonly abused substances, the risks they pose to children, and where children acquire them. Once you know that, the **most important** thing you can do is to talk with your children rather than leave their drug and alcohol education to a random website or television sitcom. We'll discuss ways to have those conversations in Section 4.

TOBACCO

Whether smoked or chewed, nicotine is one of the most highly addictive drugs used in today's society—and the addiction is extremely hard to break. The good news is that tobacco use and experimentation with tobacco products have declined for middle school and high school students compared to previous generations,[18] according to the Centers for Disease Control and Prevention (CDC). Even so, over 19 percent of high school students were cigarette smokers in 2009, as were 5.2 percent of middle school students.[19] In 2009, every day, about 3,800 teens began smoking and 1,100 become regular smokers.[20] It is illegal in all states to sell tobacco products to persons under age 18. Smoking continues to be the single leading preventable cause of death and disease in the United States,[21] so it's important to establish your household as one where tobacco use is **NOT** tolerated.

> Many tobacco products are easily recognized: a cigar, a pack of cigarettes, or a container of smokeless tobacco (chewing tobacco or snuff). However, some companies have developed products that you may not know about and that are specifically aimed at young people. One tobacco product you may not be familiar with is called a bidi cigarette, which consists of tobacco wrapped in leaves of plants that are native to Asia. Typically tied on one or both ends with string, bidis come in flavors such as chocolate, mango, vanilla, lemon-lime, mint, pineapple, and cherry—flavors that appeal to young smokers.

Though not widely used (estimates are that about 3 percent of current high school students smoke bidi cigarettes), they are especially dangerous because they contain more than three times the amount of nicotine and carbon monoxide as traditional cigarettes and five times as much tar as cigarettes.

> Another method of using tobacco that you may not recognize is with a hookah. Sometimes called a water pipe, hookahs are used to smoke specially made tobacco that is available in a variety of flavors (e.g., apple, mint, cherry, chocolate, coconut, licorice, cappuccino, and watermelon). Hookah smoking is typically practiced in groups, with the same mouthpiece passed from person to person. While used in Persia and India for centuries, today, hookah cafés are gaining popularity around

the globe, including in the United States. In recent years, there has been an increase in hookah use around the world, most notably among youths.

> Also, smokeless tobacco is *not* a safe alternative to smoking, as it contains 28 cancer-causing agents (*carcinogens*), and adolescent smokeless tobacco users are more likely than nonusers to become adult cigarette smokers.[22] According to the 2011 MTF survey, 3.5 percent of eighth-graders, 6.6 percent of 10th-graders, and 8.3 percent of 12th-graders reported smokeless tobacco use during the past month.[23] These products may be attractive because they are flavored and produce less saliva than previous versions (so no one has to know you are using them).

Regardless of the product, teenagers who use tobacco are at risk of developing cancer, heart and lung disease, and many other diseases associated with smoking. The best ways to prevent your child from smoking are to (1) not smoke, and (2) not allow smoking in your home. Teens whose parents smoke are almost three times as likely to use tobacco themselves.[24] And remember, teens who smoke cigarettes are much more likely to use marijuana than those who have never smoked.

If you discover your children are already using tobacco, remind them that it is illegal for them to purchase tobacco products, and let them know you expect them to quit immediately. Be firm but supportive, as breaking a tobacco addiction can be extremely difficult, but continue to emphasize that quitting is imperative. If necessary, your family physician may prescribe medication to help break the habit or direct your child to support programs for quitting smoking.

ALCOHOL

Why have we included alcohol in a book about drugs? Alcohol *is* a drug. It's illegal for kids under 21 (in most states) to use it,[25] and it's **dangerous**. Kids who drink are more likely to be victims of violent crimes, have serious problems in school, and be involved in drinking-related traffic crashes.[26] Underage alcohol use is more likely to kill young people than all illegal drugs combined.[27]

As children approach adolescence, they want to fit in with their peers, and alcohol is a common drug of choice. You may think your child hasn't begun drinking yet. You may be right, but by the time they reach the eighth grade, nearly half of all adolescents have had a least one drink, and over 20 percent report having been drunk. The trend continues as students enter high school. A recent national study of 12th-graders showed that nearly a third of these students binge drink, which was defined as drinking at least five drinks at one time within the last two weeks.[28]

Using alcohol is a poor choice that likely leads to more poor choices for young people. Seventy-five percent of teens reported that the teens they knew who drank alcohol or used illegal drugs were more likely to engage in sexual activity.[29]

Alcohol affects the mind and body in unpredictable ways, and teens lack the judgment and coping skills to handle alcohol wisely. As a result[30]

> Alcohol-related traffic crashes are a major cause of death among young people. Alcohol use also is linked with teen deaths by drowning, suicide, and homicide.

> Teens who use alcohol are more likely to be sexually active at earlier ages, to have sexual intercourse more often, and to have

The risk of alcohol poisoning is also increased when teens drink alcohol along with energy drinks or consume energy drinks that contain alcohol. These drinks, which are on most grocery store shelves, are loaded with caffeine, other plant-based stimulants, and other additives.

unprotected sex than teens who do not drink.

> Young people who drink are more likely than others to be victims of violent crimes, including rape, aggravated assault, and robbery.

> Teens who drink are more likely to have problems with school work and school conduct.

> The majority of boys and girls who drink tend to binge (five or more drinks on an occasion for boys; four or more on an occasion for girls).

> A person who begins drinking as a young teen is four times more likely to develop alcohol dependence than someone who waits until adulthood to use alcohol.

What can you do? Well, you can restrict your child's access to the liquor stored in your home. In a 2011 survey,[31] teens whose parent(s) had consumed alcohol in the previous 30 days were more than twice as likely to say they could get alcohol in an hour or less (32 percent vs. 14 percent). If you keep alcohol in your home, keep track of the supply, and lock it up if possible.

Your disapproval of underage drinking is key to keeping your child sober. Don't underestimate your power as a parent—let your kids know what you expect by talking with them and by setting an example for them. Keeping quiet may give your children the impression that you think their drinking is okay.

Alcohol Poisoning

Myth #2 at the front of this publication mentioned that alcohol poisoning, which can happen the very first time someone drinks alcohol, can cause serious brain damage or death. A person (of any age) who drinks enough alcohol will eventually get sleepy and pass out. Particularly troubling is that if the person consumed alcohol rapidly, the level of alcohol in the bloodstream (called *blood alcohol content* or BAC) will continue to rise even after the person passes out. A high BAC suppresses natural reflexes, such as the ability to gag, so a person who vomits while passed out can literally choke and die. And a person who survives may suffer irreversible brain damage.

The risk of alcohol poisoning is also increased when teens drink alcohol along with energy drinks or consume energy drinks that contain alcohol. These drinks, which are on most grocery store shelves, are loaded with caffeine, other plant-based stimulants, and other additives. They are very popular and regularly consumed by 31 percent of 12- to 17-year-olds and 34 percent of 18- to 24-year-olds.[32] But when mixed with alcohol, caffeine masks the depressant in the alcohol, and people feel more alert and sober than they really are. They eventually go to bed—not realizing they have consumed a lethal dose of alcohol. A person who appears to be sleeping it off may be in real danger. More than 13,000 ER visits related to the highly

caffeinated drinks were reported in 2009; nearly half the emergencies occurred after beverages were mixed with alcohol or other drugs.[33]

Discuss the signs of alcohol poisoning with your children. Those signs include

> mental confusion

> stupor

> coma (or inability to be roused)

> vomiting

> seizures

> slow breathing or irregular breathing

> hypothermia (low body temperature)

> bluish skin color and/or paleness

If you suspect someone has alcohol poisoning, call 911 immediately.

HOUSEHOLD PRODUCTS: INHALANTS

Items in your cabinets at home may be enough for your child to get high—even items that you might not consider "drugs." Hundreds of products such as nail polish remover, cleaning fluid, hair spray, gasoline, spray paint, and the propellant in aerosol whipped cream contain chemicals that youths inhale to get high. Because these inhalants are easily available, they are often among the first drugs that young adolescents abuse.[34]

Why do children in this group experiment with inhalants? They're cheap. They're available. And most important, kids don't understand the dangers of inhalant use—that these inhalants starve the body of oxygen and can cause unconsciousness, severe damage to the brain and nervous system, and even death.

Inhalants generally fall into the following categories.

Volatile solvents are liquids that vaporize at room temperature. They

MEET SETH BRAMLEY

When Seth Bramley changed high schools in 10th grade, his new friends introduced him to alcohol and marijuana. That was also when he started to get into trouble. He and his mom thought it would be a good idea to change his environment and go to Arkansas to live with his dad. After a month, Seth's dad caught him smoking pot and sent him back home.

Seth realized that he had a drug problem, and he went to rehab (rehab means a drug abuse treatment facility). He did well, although it was very hard on him and he wanted a different program. He went to another rehab, graduated, and went to a halfway house. But the grip of addiction was still there. He told his mom, "Mom, I so much want to live ... I don't want to get high, but I just can't stop." On Father's Day, Seth came home for a visit and got high with friends.

Giving up wasn't Seth's way, so he told his mom he wanted to get his life back on track and go back to southern California to live with his grandmother. He was there for two days. He went to dinner with his mom and grandmother on Friday night. On Sunday morning, he died after "bagging" a can of shaving gel. He was 19 years old.

Would you have pursued further rehabilitation options in this case? Rehab is often not a one-time event. Do not give up hope if your child relapses after being in a drug treatment facility. Continue to work with your physicians, counselors, and other substance abuse professionals to seek appropriate treatment and follow-up care.

SHOULD YOU SCREEN YOUR CHILD FOR DRUGS?

The American Academy of Pediatrics (AAP) suggested in 2011 that all adolescents should be screened for alcohol, tobacco, and other drug use at every office visit because their vulnerability to addiction is particularly high, as are risk-taking and injuries related to alcohol, tobacco, and drug use.[35] Screening may consist of the pediatrician simply asking your child about the use of alcohol, marijuana, or anything else to get high. Depending on the answers, the pediatrician can provide positive feedback, advice, or a treatment referral when needed. This type of screening is one indicator of whether you are on the right track with keeping your child drug free.

are found in many easily available products such as paint thinners and removers, dry-cleaning fluids, degreasers, gasoline, glues, correction fluids, and felt-tip markers.

Aerosols are sprays that contain propellants and solvents, such as spray paints, deodorant and hair sprays, vegetable oil sprays for cooking, and fabric protector sprays.

Gases include medical anesthetics (ether, chloroform, and others), as well as gases used in household or commercial products. Nitrous oxide—the most abused of these gases—is found in whipped cream dispensers and products that boost octane levels in racing cars. Other products containing gases include butane lighters, propane tanks, and refrigerants.

Nitrites, unlike most other inhalants, act directly on the central nervous system to dilate blood vessels and relax the muscles. Nitrites are now prohibited by the Consumer Product Safety Commission but can still be found, typically labeled as video head cleaner, room odorizer, leather cleaner, or liquid aroma.

People who abuse inhalants breathe in the vapors through their nose or mouth by

› Sniffing or snorting fumes from containers

› Spraying aerosols directly into the nose or mouth

› Sniffing or inhaling fumes from substances sprayed or placed into a plastic or paper bag ("bagging")

› "Huffing" from an inhalant-soaked rag stuffed in the mouth

› Inhaling from balloons filled with nitrous oxide

The lungs absorb the inhaled chemicals into the bloodstream very quickly, and the user feels effects similar to those produced by alcohol (e.g., slurred speech, lack of coordination, euphoria, dizziness). But because the high lasts only a few minutes, people often inhale repeatedly for several hours.

Inhalants can damage brain cells by preventing them from receiving enough oxygen. Repeat abusers may have difficulty learning, carrying on conversations, and solving problems. Long-term inhalant users can experience muscle spasms and permanent difficulty walking, bending, and talking. Inhalants can be addictive and can cause heart damage, liver failure, and muscle weakness.

Prolonged sniffing of these highly concentrated chemicals can cause irregular or rapid heart rhythms, and can lead to heart failure and death within minutes. High concentrations of inhalants also can cause death from suffocation when the inhalant vapor takes the place of oxygen in the lungs and brain, causing breathing to stop.

OVER-THE-COUNTER (OTC) MEDICATIONS

An over-the-counter (OTC) medication is a drug sold without a prescription, such as a medicine for a cold or cough. Many of these medications contain dextromethorphan (DXM), and the products are very effective when used as directed. But sadly, young people are abusing this type of OTC drug by drinking cough and cold medications (e.g., Robitussin, Coricidin, and Ny-quil) either alone or with soft drinks or alcohol. Gelcaps and pills are swallowed or crushed and put into drinks.

Products containing DXM are available over-the-counter in pharmacies and grocery stores; DXM is also sold on the Internet. Some websites even tell users how much to take, what drugs to combine it with, and how to extract the DXM from cough medicines—some even sell a powder form of DXM for snorting. These products are easy enough to get such that one in 10 teens (10 percent or 2.4 million) report abusing cough medicine to get high.[36]

As part of CASA's 2011 national online survey, teens aged 12–17 were asked if they knew a friend or classmate who used OTC medicines to get high. Those who answered YES were asked if they knew **more than one** friend or classmate who used OTC medicines to get high. An astounding 70 percent said they did![37]

Labels on these medications warn of the side effects when taken in high doses, including confusion, dizziness, double or blurred vision, slurred speech, loss of physical coordination, rapid heartbeat, drowsiness, and disorientation. The problem is that teens rarely read labels and don't understand the danger in using

OTC medications. According to the results of a Partnership for a Drug Free America survey, more than half of teens didn't think using cough medicines to get high was risky.[38]

Because OTC medications are so widely available, it's important to know which ones are stored in your home and their potential side effects. More importantly, keep **all** medications—particularly cough and cold medicines—in a secure location (such as a locked cabinet) where they aren't accessible to young people.

PRESCRIPTION MEDICATIONS

For decades, people have taken prescription drugs—prescribed by a doctor or dentist and dispensed by a pharmacist—to relieve a host of symptoms. The number of prescription drugs available today is mind-boggling, as is the number of young people abusing these drugs. It is sometimes their first introduction to drug use.

> Research indicates that as many as one in five teens say they have taken a prescription drug without having a prescription for it themselves.[39]

> Every day, 2,100 teenagers use a prescription drug for non-medical use for the first time.[40]

One reason for this increase is that many teens mistakenly believe prescription drugs are safer than "street drugs" because they are *medicine* prescribed by a physician. According to a Partnership for a Drug Free America survey, two in five teens felt prescription medicines, even if not prescribed by a doctor, were "much safer" to use than illegal drugs.[41] And nearly one-third of those teens believed there was "nothing wrong" with using prescription medicines without a prescription "once in a

while." But when used to get high, prescription medications are every bit as dangerous as "street drugs." Overdosing (especially on prescription pain relievers such as Vicodin, Percocet, Loritab, and others) can be fatal.

Another reason for the rising rates of use is that prescription drugs are so readily available. The majority of teens get prescription drugs from the medicine cabinets of family, friends, and acquaintances.[42] Some young people traffic among themselves—handing out or selling extra Ritalin or Adderall pills of their own or that they've acquired or stolen; some get theirs illicitly from doctors, pharmacists, or online.

What drugs in your medicine cabinet can potentially be abused?

> Also known as *opioids*, **narcotics** dull the senses and relieve pain. Hydrocodone products are the most frequently prescribed

MEET JASON SURKS

Jason Surks was 19 and in his second year of college, studying to be a pharmacist, when he died of an overdose of pills. After his death, his parents discovered that he had been ordering pills from an Internet pharmacy in Mexico.

His mother, Linda, writes: "I think back to the last several months of my son's life, trying to identify any signs I might have missed. I remember that during his first year in college, I discovered an unlabeled pill bottle in his room. I took the pills to my computer and identified them as a generic form of Ritalin. When I confronted Jason, he told me he got them from a friend who'd been prescribed the medication. He wanted to see if they would help him with his problem focusing in school. He promised he would stop using the drug. But as a pre-pharmacy major, maybe he felt he knew more about these substances than he actually did and had a 'professional curiosity' about them."

As a parent, would you have allowed Jason to self-medicate? If your child—regardless of age—feels there is a medical need for a prescription medication, see your family physician or pediatrician. Taking pharmaceuticals prescribed for someone else is illegal and can be deadly.

opioids in the United States, and they are the most abused narcotic in this country.[43] Found in pharmaceutical drugs like Vicodin, Lorcet, and Lortab, Hydrocodone is used for the treatment of moderate to moderately severe pain.

› **Stimulants** speed up the body's systems. This class of drugs includes prescription drugs such as amphetamines (Adderall and Dexedrine), methylphenidate (Concerta and Ritalin), and diet aids (such as Didrex, Bontril, Preludin, Fastin, Adipex P, Ionomin, and Meridia).

› **Barbiturates** depress the central nervous system. They have been used as sedatives, hypnotics, anesthetics, and anticonvulsants. Abusers prefer the short-acting and intermediate barbiturates such as Amytal and Seconal.

› **Benzodiazepines** are depressants that produce sedation, induce sleep, relieve anxiety and muscle spasms, and prevent seizures. The most common benzodiazepines

are the prescription drugs Valium, Xanax, Halcion, Ativan, and Klonopin. Others include ProSom, Dalmane, Restoril, Versed, Librium, Tranxene, Paxipam, Serax, Centrax, and Doral. Ambien and Sonata are sedative-hypnotic medications approved for the short-term treatment of insomnia and that share many of the properties of benzodiazepines.

Teens take these drugs for a variety of reasons. Some take stimulants (such as those used to treat attention deficit hyperactivity disorder, or ADHD) to give them additional energy and an ability to focus when studying or taking tests. Some try pain relievers to cope with stress. Others abuse prescription amphetamines to lose weight or prescription anabolic steroids to bulk up. And, sadly, some simply take prescription medicine to get high.

Many parents don't talk with their children about the non-medical use of prescription drugs—because parents don't realize how popular these drugs are or how dangerous they can be,

particularly when taken with over-the-counter medication and/or alcohol. In fact, one national study showed that 28 percent of parents have taken a prescription drug without having a prescription for it themselves.[44] This sets a dangerous example for kids, and it is illegal.

Just as with OTC medications, talk to your teens about the dangers of abusing prescription drugs, and safeguard your own medicines by keeping prescription drugs in a secure place—preferably a locked cabinet—and monitoring the number of pills you have. Regularly dispose of expired or unused medications in a safe manner by removing the substance from its original container, mixing it with an undesirable substance (such as used coffee grounds or kitty litter), and placing it in a sealable bag, empty can, or other container prior to disposal in household trash. Another alternative is to drop the substance at a medication "take-back" program in your community.

Finally, report suspicious online pharmacies. If you or your teen is aware of someone distributing prescription drugs or selling them on a suspicious Internet pharmacy site, call the DEA hotline at 1-877-792-2873. It is open around the clock, 365 days per year.

Anabolic Steroids

Weightlifters, football players, and other athletes often use anabolic steroids illegally to bulk up. They take the drug in pill form, apply it to the skin, or (more commonly) inject it into muscles with a hypodermic needle.

Abusing anabolic steroids can pose serious risks. A 2010 study funded by the National Institute on Drug Abuse (NIDA) asked teens if they had ever tried steroids—even once. Only 1.1 percent of eighth-graders, 1.6 percent of 10th-graders, and 2.0 percent of

12th-graders responded that they had.[45] Still, talk with your child about the dangers of using them.

In some individuals, steroid use can cause dramatic mood swings, increased feelings of hostility, impaired judgment, and increased levels of aggression (often referred to as "roid rage"). Other side effects can include stunted growth, accelerated puberty changes, jaundice, fluid retention, high blood pressure, increases in LDL (bad cholesterol) and decreases in HDL (good cholesterol), severe acne, trembling, and liver and kidney tumors. Abusers who inject steroids may share contaminated needles, putting them at risk for viral infections such as HIV/AIDS or hepatitis B or C.

Steroid abuse can cause extreme mood swings that include depression, paranoia, and extreme irritability. While it is important to stop using anabolic steroids, some users experience dangerous withdrawal symptoms when they stop, including depression, which sometimes leads to suicide attempts.

STREET DRUGS

"Street drugs" in this publication means illegal drugs such as marijuana, cocaine, Ecstasy, methamphetamine, and heroin. All street drugs are illegal, and the penalties for possessing them can be harsh.

Marijuana

Marijuana use among adolescents is on the rise after a decade of decline.[46] Part of this increase appears to be because adolescents don't accurately perceive the risks associated with marijuana use. This may be because of conflicting messages—they hear and read about drug legalization, decriminalization, and the use of medical marijuana.

As with other substances, young people tend to form opinions based on what their parents think and do. For example, recent studies and surveys revealed that

> Marijuana use was much less prevalent among youths who perceived strong parental disapproval for trying marijuana or hashish once or twice.[47]

> Compared to teens whose parent never used marijuana, teens whose parent has used marijuana are two-and-a-half times as likely to have also used it.[48]

It seems that marijuana is easy to obtain. In the 2010 national CASA survey, 58 percent of teens who said they can get marijuana do so by calling a cell phone or by sending a text message; 57 percent said they simply ask for it face to face; and 14 percent said they use websites like Facebook or MySpace.[49]

MEET TAYLOR HOOTEN

Taylor Hooten died at age 17. It took a while for his parents to connect Taylor's recent weight and muscle increases with his uncharacteristic mood swings and violent, angry behavior. He'd been using a cocktail of steroids and other hormones to bulk up, and the drugs were wreaking havoc on his body and emotions. Taylor went to his room and hanged himself.

---

*What would you have done if Taylor were your son? Frequent extreme or unusual physical or emotional changes that affect your child's relationships, health, academic performance, or other aspects of life are **not** normal. Those uncharacteristic changes may be your red flag that your child is addicted to drugs or alcohol.*

In the 2011 MTF survey, one in four—25 percent—of the 47,000 teens surveyed said they had used marijuana during the last year. The survey, which polled students nationwide in the eighth, 10th, and 12th grades, also found that nearly one in 15 high school students used pot on a daily or near-daily basis!

Marijuana use and addiction can't be taken lightly. Approximately 1.1 million drug-related treatment admissions to publicly funded facilities occurred in 2009 (the latest year for which data are available). Of those, 31 percent reported marijuana as their primary drug of choice.[50]

Bottom line: marijuana is a drug, it is dangerous, and it is illegal.

Stimulants

Stimulants are drugs that speed up the body's systems. Examples of illicit stimulants include cocaine, methamphetamine, and Ecstasy.

> *Cocaine* comes in two forms. Powder cocaine is made from the leaf of the coca plant and is usually snorted or injected into a vein with a needle, while crack is a form of cocaine that is often smoked in a glass pipe. Physiological effects of cocaine include increased blood pressure and heart rate, dilated pupils, insomnia, and loss of appetite. The widespread abuse of pure street cocaine has led to many severe adverse health consequences such as cardiac arrhythmias, ischemic heart conditions, sudden cardiac arrest, convulsions, strokes, or death. Additionally, cocaine is highly addictive.

> *Ecstasy* (or MDMA) is both a stimulant and psychedelic—and it is highly addictive. Researchers have determined that many Ecstasy tablets contain additional drugs or drug combinations that can be harmful.[51] Other drugs are often sold as Ecstasy, which can lead to overdose and death when the user takes additional doses to obtain the desired effect. Ecstasy is usually taken in pill form and often combined with alcohol and/or other drugs. In high doses, MDMA can interfere with the body's ability to regulate temperature, which can then result in liver, kidney, and cardiovascular system failure—or death.

> *Methamphetamine* (or "meth") is a powerful stimulant derived from amphetamine. It comes in clear crystals or powder and easily dissolves in water or alcohol. Meth is sometimes made using inexpensive over-the-counter ingredients such as drain cleaner, battery acid, and antifreeze—definitely **NOT** the kinds of products you want your child to consume! Meth is swallowed, snorted, injected, or smoked. "Ice" (or crystal meth) is a large, usually clear crystal of high purity that is smoked, like crack, in a glass pipe. Like other stimulants, meth is highly addictive.

Heroin

Heroin is typically sold as a white or brownish powder or as the black sticky substance known on the streets as "black tar heroin" that can be injected, smoked, or sniffed/snorted. Because most street heroin is cut with other drugs or with substances like sugar or starch, heroin users do not know the actual strength of the drug or its true contents. This puts them at a high risk of overdose or death. Heroin users develop a tolerance to the drug, making it particularly addictive.

When teens were asked in the national 2011 CASA survey on substance abuse if they knew a friend or classmate who used illegal drugs like acid, Ecstasy, meth, cocaine, or heroin, two out of five (42 percent) said they did. Of those who knew a friend or classmate who used such drugs, 73 percent said they knew more than one who did.

FAMILY OUTRAGED AT TEENS' EASY ACCESS TO DRUGS[52]

Late in 2011, a young girl in Indiana nearly died, according to her parents, after taking a "designer drug" called "bath salts." She was with a group of teens who all tried the drug that's making its rounds across the country.

Her mother was shocked. "I had heard a little bit about it, didn't know much about it. I assumed bath salts—like a lot of people—is what you put in a bath tub, what you buy in a store." In fact, it's a chemical compound made to be taken as a drug, but packages often indicate that it's not for consumption.

"You just go into the gas station, if you're 18, and you tell them what you want, they'll give it to you," the girl explained. "And I guess if you're not, you can just tell them a code word, and they'll give it to you."

The young girl said she didn't know the dangers of bath salts but was curious, so she tried it. Afterward, she said, "I had no idea where I was or what I was saying or what was even going on around me." In a cell phone video, her mother shows the teen at the hospital, rocking incessantly and crying.

Synthetic stimulants sold as "Bath Salts." *DEA photos.*

SYNTHETIC DRUGS

Synthetic drugs have emerged as a serious problem during the past few years because they are marketed openly and sold as legal alternatives to illegal drugs. Synthetic drugs generally fall into two categories:

> *Synthetic cannabinoids* (synthetic marijuana, sometimes called K2/Spice). Often marketed as incense, K2/Spice and other synthetic marijuana products are sold primarily in paraphernalia shops, smoke shops, adult book stores, convenience stores, and online. In the 2011 MTF national survey, researchers asked 12th-grade students about synthetic marijuana and were surprised to learn that 11 percent of the high school seniors surveyed had tried the substance. Emergency room physicians report that individuals who use these types of products experience dangerous side effects, including convulsions, anxiety attacks, dangerously elevated heart rates, increased blood pressure, vomiting, and disorientation. Synthetic cannabinoids are sprayed on plant material that provides a vehicle for the most common route of administration—smoking (using a pipe, a water pipe, or rolling the drug-spiked plant material in cigarette papers). Because the ingredients are unregulated and often unknown, synthetic marijuana can be much more dangerous than plant-based marijuana. Some of the chemicals in synthetic marijuana have been reclassified as controlled substances, which makes them illegal.

> *Synthetic stimulants* (sometimes called Ivory Wave or Vanilla Sky). Often marketed as bath salts or plant food, synthetic stimulants are sold as legal alternatives to cocaine, amphetamine, Ecstasy, and methcathinone. Much like K2/Spice, they are sold in smoke shops, paraphernalia shops, convenience stores, adult bookstores, gas stations, and online. Overdoses have resulted in emergency room visits, hospitalizations, and severe psychotic episodes, some of which have led to violent outbursts, self-inflicted wounds, and at least one suicide. Abusers of bath salt products have reported that they experienced chest pain, increased blood pressure, increased heart rate, agitation, panic attacks, hallucinations, extreme paranoia, and delusions. Users of bath salt products self-administer the drugs by snorting the powder, smoking it, or injecting themselves intravenously. Some of the chemicals in bath salts have been classified as controlled substances which make them illegal.

These synthetic drugs are **extremely** dangerous. Calls to poison control centers have risen dramatically since these products hit the United States, as users of synthetic marijuana and synthetic stimulants can experience severe adverse effects.[53] Nationwide, more than 4,000 calls about bath salts came in to poison centers during the first seven months of 2011—up from 303 calls in all of 2010.[54]

[18] Centers for Disease Control and Prevention. Morbidity and Mortality Weekly Reports. *Morbidity and Mortality Weekly Report, Tobacco Use Among Middle and High School Students. United States. 2000-2009.* Volume 59, Number 33, August 27, 2010.

[19] Ibid.

[20] *Results from the 2010 National Survey on Drug Use and Health: Summary of National Findings.*

[21] *Morbidity and Mortality Weekly Report, Tobacco Use Among Middle and High School Students.*

[22] Office on Smoking and Health, National Center for Chronic Disease Prevention and Health Promotion, Centers for Disease Control and Prevention. *Smoking and Tobacco Use Fact Sheet: Smokeless Tobacco Facts.* Last updated August 4, 2011.

[23] *Monitoring the Future national results on adolescent drug use: Overview of key findings, 2011.*

[24] *National Survey of American Attitudes on Substance Abuse XVI: Teens and Parents.*

[25] Alcohol Policy Information System. State Profiles of Underage Drinking Laws. Accessed September 21, 2012, **www.alcoholpolicy.niaaa.nih.gov/State_Profiles_of_Underage_Drinking_Laws.html**.

[26] National Institutes of Health. National Institute on Alcohol Abuse and Alcoholism. *Make a Difference – Talk To Your Child About Alcohol.* NIH Publication No. 06-4314. Revised 2009.

[27] National Institutes of Health. National Institute on Alcohol Abuse and Alcoholism. *Underage Drinking – A Growing Health Care Concern.* Accessed September 21, 2012. **http://pubs.niaaa.nih.gov/publications/PSA/underagepg2.htm**.

[28] Ibid.

[29] *National Survey of American Attitudes on Substance Abuse XV: Teens and Parents.*

[30] *Make a Difference – Talk To Your Child About Alcohol.*

[31] *National Survey of American Attitudes on Substance Abuse XVI: Teens and Parents.*

[32] Centers for Disease Control and Prevention. *Alcohol and Public Health Fact Sheet: Caffeinated Alcoholic Beverages.* Last updated July 10, 2010. Accessed September 21, 2012, **www.cdc.gov/alcohol/fact-sheets/cab.htm**.

[33] Center for Behavioral Health Statistics and Quality Substance Abuse and Mental Health Services Administration. *The DAWN Report: Emergency Department Visits Involving Energy Drinks.* November 22, 2011. Accessed September 21, 2012, **www.samhsa.gov/data/2k11/WEB_DAWN_089/WEB_DAWN_089_HTML.pdf**.

[34] National Institute on Drug Abuse. NIDA for Teens, The Science Behind Drugs Abuse. *Facts on Drugs: Inhalants.* Last updated March 2012. Accessed September 21, 2012, **http://teens.drugabuse.gov/facts/facts_inhale1.php**.

[35] AAP Committee on Substance Abuse Pediatrics. 2011. *Substance use screening, brief intervention, and referral to treatment for pediatricians.* DOI: 10.1542/peds.2011-1754.

[36] Drug Enforcement Administration. *Prescription for Disaster – How Teens Abuse Medicine. A DEA Resource for Parents.* December 8, 2008. Accessed September 21, 2012, **www.getsmartaboutdrugs.com/Files/File/DEApillbook_1_5_08.pdf**.

[37] *National Survey of American Attitudes on Substance Abuse XVI: Teens and Parents.*

[38] *Prescription for Disaster – How Teens Abuse Medicine.*

[39] *Preventing Teen Abuse of Prescription Drugs Fact Sheet.* The Partnership at DrugFree.org. 2010. Accessed September 21, 2012, **www.drugfree.org/wp-content/uploads/2010/10/Preventing-Teen-Abuse-of-Prescription-Drugs-Fact-Sheet-2draft-Cephalon-sponsored.pdf**.

[40] *Results from the 2010 National Survey on Drug Use and Health: Summary of National Findings.*

[41] *Prescription for Disaster – How Teens Abuse Medicine.*

[42] *Preventing Teen Abuse of Prescription Drugs.*

[43] *Prescription for Disaster – How Teens Abuse Medicine.*

[44] *Preventing Teen Abuse of Prescription Drugs.*

[45] Johnston, L. D., O'Malley, P. M., Bachman, J. G., & Schulenberg, J. E. *Monitoring the Future national survey results on drug use, 1975–2010: Volume I, Secondary school students. Overview of Key Findings.* National Institute on Drug Abuse. Ann Arbor: Institute for Social Research. The University of Michigan. 2010.

[46] U.S. Department of Justice, National Drug Intelligence Center. *National Drug Threat Assessment 2011.* August 2011. Accessed September 21, 2012, **www.justice.gov/ndic/pubs44/44849/44849p.pdf**.

[47] *Results from the 2010 National Survey on Drug Use and Health, Summary of National Findings.*

[48] *National Survey of American Attitudes on Substance Abuse XVI: Teens and Parents.*

[49] *National Survey of American Attitudes on Substance Abuse XV: Teens and Parents.*

[50] *National Drug Threat Assessment 2011.*

[51] Drug Enforcement Administration. *Drug Fact Sheet: Ecstacy or MDMA Overview.* Accessed September 21, 2012, **www.justthinktwice.com/drugs/ecstasy_or_mdma.html**.

[52] Miller, Daniel. *Family outraged at teens' easy access to drugs.* LIN Television Corporation at WishTV.com. Published October 31, 2011. Updated November 1, 2011. Accessed September 21, 2012, **www.wishtv.com/dpp/news/local/hamilton_county/family-outraged-at-teens-easy-access-to-drugs**.

[53] *National Drug Threat Assessment 2011.*

[54] National Institute on Drug Abuse. NIDA for Teens, The Science Behind Drugs Abuse. The Sara Bellum Blog. *Keep "Bath Salts" in the Tub.* Posted September 16, 2011. Accessed September 21, 2012, **http://teens.drugabuse.gov/blog/bath-salts-tub**.

SECTION 3:
WHY DO KIDS USE DRUGS?

Which children are at risk for drug and/or alcohol use? *All of them!*

RISK FACTORS AND PROTECTIVE FACTORS

Children are more likely to try drugs or develop abuse issues because of *risk factors*—circumstances or events that increase a person's chances for drug abuse. The more risk factors present, the more likely a child may be to develop problems from drug use. Those with a higher risk include children who are

> Failing in school

> Victims of bullying (including cyberbullying)

> Experiencing low self-esteem

> Living with an addicted family member

> Residing in a community with a high tolerance for smoking, drinking, or drug use among youths

> Attending a school without strict rules that address tobacco, alcohol, or drugs and consistent enforcement for breaking those rules

Some kids have a lower risk of drug use and abuse because of *protective factors*. A protective factor is a preventative measure, of sorts—something that makes a child less likely to use drugs.

Protective factors include

> Experiencing a strong bond with a parent or caregiver

> Having high self-esteem

> Having parents who talk regularly with their child about drugs

> Being active in faith-based organizations, or school, athletic, or community activities

> Spending time around positive role models who don't use tobacco, drugs, or alcohol

> Being involved in healthy activities that involve managed risk, such as rock climbing, karate, or camping

> Living in a community that offers youths activities where drugs and alcohol are prohibited

> Attending a school with an effective drug education program and a no-tolerance policy for alcohol and drugs

Risk and protective factors are present in homes, schools, and communities. As a parent, it is impossible to control **all** risk and protective factors. However, you can control the risk and protective factors in your home and work to change others in your child's environment. Ideally, it's not enough to simply "balance" risk and protective factors. You want the scales weighted heavily in your favor! To increase your odds of that, (1) remove as many risk factors as you possibly can, and (2) add as many protective factors as you can.

RISK FACTORS

Some risk factors we can control; others we can't. But we first need to know what we are up against—what influences and temptations our children face and what we can do to shift the odds in favor of a drug-free lifestyle.

Academics

How well children are doing in school might be an indicator of whether or not they will use drugs.[55] Students with higher grades are significantly less likely to have engaged in behaviors such as

> Alcohol use

> Binge drinking

> Trying alcohol for the first time before age 13

> Marijuana use

> Taking prescription drugs to get high

> Using Ecstasy

A national CDC survey found that only 32 percent of ninth- through 12th-grade students with mostly A's used alcohol, while 62 percent of students with mostly D's or F's used alcohol.[56] Kids who don't feel they are "making the grade" in school likely suffer from low self-esteem, which further increases their vulnerability to try drugs. It makes sense, then, to be sure your child has every opportunity to learn and to succeed academically.

Your Own Alcohol, Tobacco, and Drug Use

Myth #5 (on page 4 of this publication) explained that some parents believe it's okay for them to use even though they tell their children not to. This can be a very touchy subject if you like to occasionally have wine with dinner or a cold beer on the weekend. With alcohol, you must drink responsibly, limiting the amount you consume. A 2012 report shows that 7.5 million children under age 18 (10.5 percent of this population) lived with a parent who experienced an alcohol use disorder in the previous year.57 Children of parents with untreated alcohol disorders are at far greater risk for developing alcohol and other problems later in their lives, so don't be afraid to seek help if you need it.

And what if you smoke? While it is legal for adults to smoke cigarettes, it isn't a habit you want to pass along to your children. If your child wants to know why you smoke, explain why you started, and explain that you have become addicted and how it has negatively affected your life. Ask your child to support your efforts to quit. Then *do it*.

At some point, your child is likely to ask, "Have you ever used drugs?" Do not be uncomfortable with the question. Instead, be honest and use the opportunity to talk with your child about the importance of avoiding drug use.

If your answer is **NO**, explain to your child how you were able to avoid temptation and peer pressure, the reasons you felt it was important, and why you are happy that you chose to do so. Talk about the opportunities you've had (relationships, college, jobs, etc.) because you resisted the temptation. Did it enable you to save money for college or to buy a home? Did it allow you to enter the military? Point out the positive things in your life that happened because you chose not to use drugs.

If your answer is YES, expand on that with why you don't want your child to do the same thing. Don't forget to include: it is illegal! You don't need to confess every single event from your past. Skip the details and explain honestly what attracted you to drugs, what you've since learned about the dangers of drugs, and why you want your child to avoid making the same mistake. Was your friend killed in an automobile accident after getting high and leaving a party? Were you denied your first job at a young age because you couldn't pass a drug test? You might say things like

> "I tried smoking pot to fit in. Now we know more about the dangers of drugs than we did then. If I could do things over, I never would have tried it. I hope you don't either."

> "I'm not proud of my mistakes, and it's hard for me to admit that I did try drugs. I'm glad you are smart enough not to make the same mistakes I made."

> "I used drugs because I was bored, but it seemed like I wanted to do them more and more. I was terrified of getting addicted to them, so I got into a drug abuse treatment program that helped me quit, but it was very hard. I've also relapsed a few times ... I hope you aren't ever in that situation."

> "I started drinking and doing drugs when I was young, and I missed a big part of growing up. I love you too much to watch you set yourself on the same path."

> "It was illegal then just like it is now, and there are serious consequences for getting caught. I would hate for you to ruin your future by doing something illegal."

If you are currently smoking marijuana or using other illegal drugs, your child will likely follow in your footsteps. As a parent, your own use affects your child's sense of acceptable behavior. Remember, you are an important role model!

It's also important for older siblings to set a good example. According to a 2011 report by CASA,[58] teens who believed their siblings have tried an illegal drug were

> More than five-and-a-half times as likely to have used tobacco

> Almost three times as likely to have used alcohol

> Six-and-a-half times as likely to have used marijuana

Genetics

If substance abuse is a persistent generational problem in your family, explain to your children that they may have inherited genes that put them at a higher risk of becoming addicted to alcohol or drugs. Using the example of a family member— or yourself—to illustrate why your children should be careful about trying alcohol or drugs makes it easier for them to understand because it involves someone they know, and they have likely witnessed troublesome issues firsthand. And if the abuser still lives in the home, get help from

your family physician, professional counselors, and/or any of the support groups shown in the Resources section at the back of this publication.

Online Environmental Risks

In past generations, drugs were often purchased from a "dealer on the corner." But today, youths can use the Internet to buy drugs, learn how to use and mix them to get high and can see what to expect from the experience. They can even view photos and videos of other people actually using drugs. All of that is possible online through *social networking*.

"Social networking" simply means interacting with others on the Internet—either on a computer or with a "smartphone" (a *smartphone* is a cell phone that can connect to the Internet). It most often occurs on websites that host blogs, chat rooms, or forums, but also on websites where people post photos and videos. Some of the best-known social networking sites today are Facebook, Twitter, MySpace, LinkedIn, and YouTube.

Monitor what your children do online by becoming acquainted with the websites they visit.

Chances are good that your child already has an account on at least one of those social networking sites. Should you be concerned? **Yes!** The 2011 CASA survey revealed that, compared to teens who, in a typical day, do not spend time on a social networking site, those who do are

> Five times as likely to use tobacco

> Three times as likely to use alcohol

> Twice as likely to use marijuana

Also alarming is that half of the teens who spend time on social networking sites have seen pictures of kids drunk, passed out, or using drugs on these sites.[59] That is a lot of visual temptation at a young age!

Unfortunately, most parents are not concerned about the risks of social networking. In fact, only about one-third of parents whose teen has a social networking page actually monitor it.[60] Clearly this means that **most parents do not**.

The Internet is a tremendous resource that has changed the world, and it can provide positive ways for teens to learn about the dangers of drug abuse. How can you ensure that your children use online privileges wisely and avoid inappropriate drug-related material?

1. Monitor what your children do online by becoming acquainted with the websites they visit.

2. Know what your children are saying on their smartphones and in chat rooms and instant messages. Kids are speaking in an abbreviated language that evolves, so stay aware of new lingo. At the time of this publication, for example

> DOC means Drug of Choice.

> PAL means Parents Are Listening.

> P911 means Parent Alert.

> The number 420 is code for marijuana.

> KPC means Keeping Parents Clueless.

3. Watch credit card and bank statements for online purchases that may indicate your child is buying drugs on the Internet.

Another sad trend to come from social networking sites is *cyberbullying*, which is a widespread problem that causes serious and lasting harm. Cyberbullying includes sending hurtful, rude, or mean text messages; spreading rumors or lies about others by e-mail or on social networking sites; and creating websites, videos, or social media profiles that embarrass, humiliate, or make fun of others.

More than 4.5 million kids have been cyberbullied, and the 2011 CASA survey on substance abuse reveals that cyberbullied teens are more than twice as likely to smoke, drink, and use marijuana. Even more alarming is that some kids ultimately kill themselves because they are embarrassed about the chronic bullying and feel helpless to stop it. Caution your children not to post secrets, photos, or anything that might be embarrassing online that can later be used against them, and encourage your children to report cyberbullying—whether it is happening to them or to someone they know.

Bottom line: social networking won't "make" your children use drugs. But spending too much time on social networking sites may increase the likelihood that they will.

Other Environmental Influences

While not interactive like social media, the power of television on young people is worth mentioning.

The same CASA survey that asked teens about social networking also asked about whether, in a typical week, they watched reality shows like *Jersey Shore, Teen Mom, 16 and Pregnant*, or any teen dramas like *Skins* or *Gossip Girl*. A third of all teens (46 percent of girls and 19 percent of boys) watch "suggestive teen programming," and the survey says those that do are likelier to use tobacco, alcohol, and marijuana.

Television shows and characters change from year to year. The ones mentioned here were popular at the time this publication was written— so stay involved by monitoring the programs your children watch, even if that simply means sitting and watching the show(s) with them. You may not like the characters or the program, but the plot and story lines can provide great ways to start conversations with your kids about what is going on in *their* lives. At the very least, you will

> One of the best protective factors you can provide is a strong parent-child bond.

know what messages your child is seeing and hearing about sex, drugs, relationships, and other social issues.

While parents can control what happens within their home, it is impossible to control every aspect of your child's environment when he or she walks out the front door. Risk factors that occur at school (such as lack of a drug education and enforcement program) or in the community (such as a high tolerance for youths who smoke) make your already challenging job even more difficult. Section 4 (*How Do I Teach My Child About Drugs?*) will present ideas for how you can become more involved in school and community efforts to reduce risk factors.

PROTECTIVE FACTORS

A number of protective factors are quite effective in helping children grow up drug-free. One of the best protective factors you can provide is a strong parent-child bond. Why? First, it tells your children that you are there 24/7 for advice. It also tells them they are valuable members of the family and that you love them, and it boosts their self-esteem so they feel good about who they are without the need for drugs or alcohol. Let's look at some of the ways to strengthen the parent-child bond.

Family Time

Make no mistake: **quality family time is a powerful protective factor**. With school activities, work, and social commitments, it's not always easy to get everyone in the family together at the same time. But family time goes beyond just getting together for meals, as mentioned in Myth #3.

> Juggle your schedule so that you can spend regular one-on-one time with each child in your family—even if it's only for short periods. This gives you and your children time to talk about whatever is going on in their lives without anyone else hearing or interrupting. For some, that may mean taking a Saturday morning bike ride. For others, it may mean chatting while you drive to or from a school activity. It may even mean talking while you're folding a load of laundry on Sunday afternoon. Whatever works for you, make the moments count. Ask your teens what is going on in their lives, and then listen to the answer. These formal or informal rituals help establish the open communication that is essential to raising drug-free children.

> Family meetings help create bonds, too. Once a week, get everyone together to talk about family issues—to celebrate what's working and resolve what isn't working. Set some simple ground rules for your meetings, such as (1) everyone gets a chance to talk, (2) no interrupting, and (3) only positive feedback is allowed. You can combine this meeting with one of your family meals—say, every Sunday night.

Open Communication

Myth #3 also mentioned the importance of being there for your child, especially during times of transition (e.g., changing schools, moving, or divorce) because the risk of drug abuse increases greatly during these transitional times.[61] As previously mentioned, family dinners and one-on-one time are also excellent ways to let your children know you will be there for them.

Another time when it's critical for you to be there is—well, any time! Assure your children that you are available any time they need to leave a place where alcohol or drugs are being used. Even if your children don't use drugs or alcohol, you don't want them riding in a vehicle with someone who does. When you can't provide transportation at a moment's notice, such as during your night shift, nominate a responsible adult who can.

Other Role Models

Parenting can feel overwhelming, especially if you are employed outside the home or are a single parent. If possible, try to find other family members or caregivers who can serve as positive role models in your child's life to ease some of your burden. Grandparents, for example, can bring a calmer, more seasoned approach to interactions with their grandchildren. They (and other extended family members) can use their positions of trust to reinforce the same lessons in self-respect and healthy living that you are trying to portray to your children. Even a neighbor or faith-based community member can serve as a positive role model if one isn't available in the family. This person can often ask more direct questions than parents can (*What kinds of drugs do kids take nowadays? What types of alcohol have you been offered at parties?*), and they might get more honest answers.

If grandparents or older family members who can serve as positive role models don't live nearby, use technology such as email or real-time video chats to bridge the miles.

Rules and Consequences

Myth #4 mentioned that youths aged 12 to 17 who believed their parents would strongly disapprove of their using substances were less likely to use that substance. That's why one critical protective factor is being consistent in your "NO drugs, NO alcohol" message. Repeat it frequently so there is no doubt about how you feel. Don't assume that your children know where you stand—they *want* you to set boundaries that help them make life choices.

Think of it this way: your child is the captain of a ship, and the seas (of life) are rough. The ship's instruments aren't wired perfectly, so your child's judgment may be clouded by inaccurate information. As much as your child *wants* to steer the ship, your child needs guidance. **YOU** can serve as a lighthouse—a beacon, of sorts—to help guide your child safely into the harbor (of adulthood).

That example may seem simplistic, but it demonstrates that growing up drug free can be hard.

› Kids receive conflicting messages from television, peers, social media, etc., and may not know which way to turn. They need you to help them, so state your position clearly. Tell your children that you forbid them to use alcohol and drugs because (1) you love them, (2) those substances are harmful for their health, and (3) those substances are illegal.

› Let them know how disappointed you'd be if you found out they were using. Rules also give your child a "way out" when tempted. If someone offers your child a cigarette, for example, your child can say, "If my mom caught me smoking, I'd be grounded and have to miss the homecoming game!" This takes the pressure off your child and shifts the blame to you, which your child may be more comfortable doing among peers.

› Establish appropriate consequences for breaking rules and consistently enforce them. Be prepared: your child may test your rules just to see if you'll follow through with consequences. By all means, do

so! This makes children feel loved and secure.

› Finally, praise your child often for respecting the rules and doing what's right. It only takes a minute a day to hug your child and say, "Thanks for being a good kid." This positive reinforcement boosts your child's self-esteem and lessens the likelihood that your child needs drugs to feel good.

Positive Activities

One reason kids may experiment with drugs is simply that they are bored. While you don't want to enroll children in every single activity, you should encourage them to find something they are interested in (e.g., sports, music, volunteer work, and faith-based activities) and to participate in it.

Being active accomplishes several things. First, it fills the empty hours after school, on weekends, or during the summer when children aren't otherwise occupied. This is especially true if you work and can't be home to monitor what your children are doing during free time. It also keeps them from spending

School connectedness is an important protective factor.

hour upon hour watching television or surfing the Internet.

Extracurricular activities help meet other needs, too. For example, involvement in activities such as rock climbing, karate, or camping fill the natural desire to engage in something risky, which may reduce their desire to use drugs. Participating in sports activities promotes a sense of team building, which shows your child that *everyone* matters. After all, you can't play football with only two people! Physical activities also encourage your child to stay healthy and drug-free, as some schools now perform drug tests on athletes.

Less athletic children may enjoy participating in art classes, attending Girls Scouts or Boy Scouts, performing volunteer work for a faith-based organization, or helping tutor younger children.

These types of positive activities have another benefit, too. They may help children discover a talent for something they didn't realize they had or a desire to pursue an occupation they never would have otherwise.

School and Community

Schools with a drug and alcohol education program and a "no tolerance" policy for substances that aligns with yours provide yet another protective factor for your children because they are hearing the same message at school as at home. Similarly, an organized anti-drug effort in the community—or at least a low tolerance for drug and alcohol abuse—will reinforce the messages you are trying to convey to your child. Again, you can't control every situation in your child's environment, but Section 4 will present ideas for how you can become more involved in school and community efforts to increase protective factors.

10 WAYS TO INCREASE YOUR CHILD'S CONNECTION TO SCHOOL

1. Encourage your child to talk openly with you, teachers, counselors, and other school staff about any ideas, needs, and worries.

2. Find out what the school expects your child to learn and the appropriate behavior for school by talking to teachers and staff, attending school meetings, and reading information the school sends home. Support these expectations at home.

3. Help your child with homework, and teach your child how to use time well. Make sure the tools—books, supplies, a quiet place to work—needed to do homework are available.

4. Read school newsletters, attend parent-teacher-student conferences, and check out the school's website to learn what is going on at the school. Encourage your child to participate in school activities.

5. Meet regularly with your child's teachers to discuss grades, behavior, and accomplishments.

6. As time allows, help in your child's classroom, attend afterschool events, or participate in a school committee, such as a health team or parent organization.

7. Offer to share important aspects of your culture with your child's class.

8. If your first language is not English, ask for materials that are translated into the language you speak at home, and ask for interpreters to help you at school events.

9. Talk with teachers and school staff to suggest simple changes that can make the school a more pleasant and welcoming place. For example, the school might decorate the eating area with student-made posters, allow families to use the school gym or other facilities during out-of-school times, or create a place in the school or on school grounds for kids and families to socialize.

10. Ask whether your school or school district provides—or could offer— programs or classes to help you become more involved in your child's academic and school life. For example, the school or school district might offer training to help you talk with your child and to help manage his or her behavior; educational programs for parents by telephone or online; and/or General Education Development (GED), English as a second language, or other classes to help you work better with your child and with the adults at school.

Courtesy of the Centers for Disease Control and Prevention

According to the CDC, *school connectedness*—the belief held by students that adults and peers in the school care about their learning as well as about them as individuals—is an important protective factor.[62] (See the sidebar above.) Research has shown that young people who feel connected to their schools are less likely to engage in many risky behaviors such as early sexual initiation; alcohol, tobacco, and other drug use; and violence and gang involvement.

Students who feel connected to their schools are also more likely to have better academic achievement, including higher grades and test scores, have better school attendance, and stay in school longer.

[55] Centers for Disease Control and Prevention. *Alcohol and Other Drug Use and Academic Achievement. 2009 National Youth Risk Behavior Survey.* June 4, 2010. Accessed September 21, 2012, www.cdc.gov/healthyyouth/health_and_academics/pdf/alcohol_other_drug.pdf.

[56] Ibid.

[57] Substance Abuse and Mental Health Services Administration. *Report shows 7.5 million children live with a parent with an alcohol use disorder.* News release dated February 16, 2012. www.samhsa.gov/newsroom/advisories/1202151415.aspx.

[58] *The Importance of Family Dinners VII.*

[59] *National Survey of American Attitudes on Substance Abuse XVI: Teens and Parents.*

[60] Ibid.

[61] National Institute on Drug Abuse. *Drugs, Brains, and Behavior - The Science of Addiction.* NIH Pub No. 10-5605. Printed April 2007. Revised February 2008, August 2010.

[62] Centers for Disease Control and Prevention. *School Connectedness: Strategies for Increasing Protective Factors Among Youth.* 2009. Accessed September 21, 2012, http://www.cdc.gov/healthyyouth/adolescenthealth/pdf/connectedness.pdf.

SECTION 4:
HOW DO I TEACH MY CHILD ABOUT DRUGS?

We've already mentioned the importance of establishing open communication with your child—but many parents find it difficult to actually talk openly about drugs. What if your child asks a question you don't know the answer to? If your children don't seem interested in drugs, should you talk to them anyway?

This section will suggest ways to talk with your child at different ages and proposes ideas for initiating conversations. It also explains the importance of being an active parent, which creates a bond that serves as a strong protective factor for your child.

EDUCATE YOURSELF

You aren't expected to know everything about parenting or drugs. And even if you did, your children— at certain rebellious stages—may not *seem* to be listening to you. They are, though, so don't let up! To effectively communicate with them about substance use, it's important that you understand what they face so you can provide advice and guidance. Reading this publication is a good first step in educating yourself about the types of drugs young people use, how they acquire them, and their negative health consequences.

No matter where you live, your children will eventually be exposed to tobacco, alcohol, or other drugs, so you need to be familiar with the substances they may encounter. The names of drugs and how they're used change constantly, so take time to review the more common drugs, paraphernalia, and street names in the **Drug Identification Chart** at the back of this publication.

EDUCATE YOUR CHILD

Another indisputable fact is that kids **will** learn about drugs. They will learn from media (television, music, movies, social networking), and they will learn from friends. But if you intervene, they will also learn from **YOU**. They will learn how you feel about drugs and how you expect them to act when tempted to use drugs. That's why it is crucial to (a) begin talking with your children about drugs at a young age, and (b) talk with them at a level they understand.

Talking to children about drugs isn't a one-time event. Instead, strive for a number of talks about substance use from preschool throughout the teenage years. Think of each talk as one "chunk" of an ongoing conversation.

A big part of talking is listening. Ask your kids what they know about marijuana. Ask if they think alcohol is dangerous. Ask what they think can happen if someone takes heroin. These attitudes are important because national drug prevention surveys have shown that the level of drug use goes

Remember: If children perceive a substance as dangerous, they may be *less* likely to use it. If they see it as not that risky, they may be *more* likely to use it.

MEET MARK BAUER

Phil Bauer writes: Since the death of my son Mark in 2004, I have asked myself many questions. What if I had talked to Mark more about the dangers of drugs? Or spent more time learning about what kids were doing at the time? If I hadn't missed the signs of addiction, would he still be alive?

A few times during Mark's teen years, we found marijuana in his room. We also knew he occasionally drank beer. I talked with him and assigned some form of punishment. I didn't see this as a life threatening behavior and didn't believe Mark had an addiction problem.

On May 27, Mark went to school, played basketball, and then went to work. He was looking forward to a camping trip and to his graduation the following week. But the next day, Mark never woke up. He died from an overdose of prescription drugs, including oxycodone, morphine, acetaminophen, and amphetamines. I never knew Mark was using prescription drugs, and I don't recall ever talking with him about the dangers.

Unfortunately, his life here on earth is over, but I hope his story will serve as a "second chance" for others.

What would you have done differently—if anything? If you suspect your child is using, talk to your family doctor or pediatrician to see about having your child assessed for substance abuse.

up as the perceived risk of using the drug goes down.[63] In other words, if young people think a particular drug is harmful, they are less likely to use that substance; if they think a particular drug isn't as harmful, they may be more likely to use it.

In the 2010 MTF survey, for example, eighth-grade students were asked *How much do you think people risk harming themselves if they smoke one or more packs of cigarettes per day?* Only 61 percent thought it was a "great risk." This is especially alarming because that is about the age when most teens are first exposed to cigarettes—and many of them apparently don't perceive smoking as risky. The same survey asked the eighth-graders *How much do you think people risk harming themselves if they try inhalants once or twice?* Only 36 percent answered that it was a "great risk." Again, students are most likely to use inhalants at about this age.

Remember: If children perceive a substance as dangerous, they may be *less* likely to use it. If they see it as not that risky, they may be *more* likely to use it. It's up to **YOU**, as a parent and role model, to make sure your children know that using tobacco, drugs, and alcohol has serious health and social effects, and it's illegal for children to use them. It's up to **YOU** to explain how USING drugs can lead to ABUSE, which can lead to ADDICTION.

BE AN INVOLVED PARENT

An excellent way to let your children know how strongly you feel about not using drugs is to *show* them by example—by being an active parent in all aspects of their lives and by not using drugs or alcohol.

Be Involved at Home

As discussed in the section on social networking, children are exposed to all kinds of information online. Be involved in their lives at home by

> Monitoring the computers in your home—and the cell phones, too, if your children use a smartphone to access the Internet.

> Knowing what types of websites they visit and who they communicate with online, as well as what they are watching on television and what music they are listening to.

> Establishing some structure for your children so that there isn't too much free time. If you work and your children will be home alone after school, assign age-appropriate household chores to accomplish and set rules about watching television or using the computer.

Be Involved in Your Child's Social Life

Regardless of your children's ages, you need to be involved in their social lives. That doesn't mean tagging along every time they leave the house, but you need to know where they are going, what they'll be doing, and what friends will be there. When your children leave home to go hang out with friends, for example, do you know who those friends are? When your child asks to attend a sleepover, do you meet and talk with the host parents to be sure the group will be chaperoned? Do your teens know the laws regarding teen driving? Did you set a time for them to return home? Do you know how many kids will be in the car? How old are they? *Who* are they?

And don't forget—when your child's friends come to *your* home, **you** are responsible for their well-being. Most states have stiff penalties for serving alcohol to minors or furnishing them drugs. It's not enough to just lock up your wine; you also need to be sure nobody in attendance brings alcohol or drugs with them to your home.

Even if you don't believe your own child is using drugs or alcohol, you should be concerned if you suspect that your teen's friends are using. In the national 2011 CASA study on substance abuse, two in five teens reported knowing at least one friend or classmate who used illegal drugs, like acid, Ecstasy, or methamphetamine; and approximately one in four teens knew at least one friend or classmate who used prescription drugs to get high.

Get to know the parents of your child's friends, too. They can be terrific allies because they also want to raise a drug-free child. Explain to the parents that your family has a strict NO use policy for tobacco, alcohol, and other drugs in your home. Exchange contact information and ask them to forbid your child's use of alcohol, tobacco, and other drugs in their home. Promise to do the same for them.

If your child is attending a party, call the parents of the other child to be sure there actually is a party taking place and ask who will be chaperoning. Explain your NO use policy to the parents and ask that no alcoholic beverages or illegal substances be present. Also, don't be afraid to go check out the party yourself. If possible, meet with other parents who have kids the same age as yours—even if it's just sharing a cup of coffee now and then or chatting during a school sporting event. It helps to find out what other parents are doing or to simply share opinions. *My child wants to go to a party where the chaperone will be a 20-year-old cousin. Are you allowing your child to go?*

Be Involved at School

Your chances of raising a drug-free child are better if school regulations

> *Get to know the parents of your child's friends, too. They can be terrific allies.*

and policies reflect the same attitude that you express at home—**tobacco, alcohol, and drug use is not acceptable**—and if those rules are enforced with consistent consequences.

> ❯ Learn the policies regarding alcohol and drug use at your child's school. For example, does the school have a student handbook that clearly states its drug and alcohol policy? Does it explain what constitutes an offense and the consequences for breaking the rules? Does it include an agreement for students and parents to sign about adhering to the policy? Is there fair and consistent punishment so that all students breaking the same rule face the same consequences?

> ❯ If there's no policy in place, schedule a meeting with the principal, arrange to meet with school board members, and/or attend PTA meetings to help develop a policy.

> ❯ Ask how drug education is provided in your child's school. Does the school use an evidence-based drug abuse curriculum or pro-

gram? Do faculty members receive regular training? Is drug education provided at age-appropriate levels throughout the year or only once during a special "drug-free" week? Does the drug education program offer educational material for parents, too?

> ❯ What procedures are in place to ensure that school activities (e.g., sports events, prom, graduation) are alcohol and drug free?

> ❯ Review all drug education materials your child brings home. Do they contain a clear message that alcohol, tobacco, and other drug use is harmful? Does your child have any questions or need clarification on anything in the material?

> ❯ Does the school have outside resources to help educate students in school? If not, work through the school to contact agencies and organizations like the Drug Enforcement Administration (**www.justice.gov/dea**); the National Guard (**http://ngbcounterdrug.ng.mil**);

DEVELOPING A COMMUNITY PREVENTION PLAN

The first step in planning a drug abuse prevention program is to assess the type of drug problem within the community and determine the level of risk factors affecting the problem. The results of this assessment can be used to raise awareness of the nature and seriousness of the community's problem and guide selection of the best prevention programs to address the problem.

Next, assessing the community's readiness for prevention can help determine additional steps needed to educate the community before launching the prevention effort. Then, a review of current programs is needed to determine existing resources and gaps in addressing community needs and to identify additional resources.

Finally, planning can benefit from the expertise of community organizations that provide youth services. Convening a meeting with leaders of these service organizations can set the stage for capturing ideas and resources to help implement and sustain research-based programs.

Prevention research suggests that a well-constructed community plan

- Identifies the specific drug and other child and adolescent problems in a community;
- Builds on existing resources (e.g., current drug abuse prevention programs);
- Develops short-term goals related to selecting and carrying out research-based prevention programs and strategies;
- Projects long-term goals so that plans and resources are available for the future; and
- Includes ongoing assessments of the prevention program.

Courtesy of NIDA[64]

Drug Abuse Resistance Education (D.A.R.E.) (www.dare.com); the Elks organization (www.elks.org); the Mothers Against Drunk Driving (MADD) (www.madd.org) and Students Against Destructive Decisions (SADD) (www.sadd.org) chapters nearest you; or the other resources listed in the back of this publication.

❯ Determine whether the school has a school nurse, a school resource officer, or a school counselor on staff or on call.

❯ Does the school have a referral system to a substance abuse treatment agency for students who need help?

❯ Find out how the school assesses its alcohol and drug problem and whether it responds to the assess-ment results by adjusting its substance abuse education program.

Finally, being involved in these efforts at your child's school serves another purpose. It lets you observe firsthand what is happening and lets you participate in shaping the drug education efforts at that school. And according to a recent CDC report, parent engagement also makes it more likely that adolescents will choose healthier behaviors, such as avoiding tobacco, alcohol, and other drug use.[65]

Be Involved in the Community

Active parenting also includes knowing what is going on in your own neighborhood. If you haven't already done so, get to know your neighbors! Ask them to report suspicious or unusual afterschool activity when you can't be home with your child. If you are a stay-at-home parent, watch for signs that your child (or other children) may be doing things they shouldn't.

On a larger scale, it's important to know what community leaders are doing to help prevent drug abuse. And if it's not enough, then get involved with that, too. For example, does your community support student-run clubs where teens can hang out, listen to music, and play sports? If not, meet with officials and/or organizations who can help you establish such places. Does the community have underage ordinances that prohibit minors from purchasing or using tobacco and alcohol? If so, are they enforced? For example, in stores where signs say the clerks ask for identification to ensure patrons are of legal age to purchase beer or cigarettes, do the clerks actually ask for an ID?

You can also check to see if an anti-drug coalition exists in your community. To find out, look online using a search engine such as Google or go to the website for the Community Anti-Drug Coalitions of America (CADCA) at www.cadca.org. There you'll find a link to email them, and a CADCA representative will contact you with details about existing community coalitions in your area or walk you through the process of starting a coalition and explain the various resources available through CADCA to help your coalition succeed. Since 1992, CADCA has offered training to local and state drug abuse prevention coalitions—teaching them how to assess their local substance abuse problems and develop a comprehensive plan to address them. Each community's drug and alcohol problems are different, of course, so CADCA brings together concerned citizens, schools, parents, businesses, healthcare providers, law enforcement, and faith-based institutions to share ideas, problems, and solutions that are unique to a particular community.

BE A GOOD ROLE MODEL

As previously mentioned, children learn what they see. This means that many of their attitudes about substance abuse will be shaped by your attitudes and your actions. If you occasionally drink alcohol, do so in moderation, and never imply that alcohol is a good way to handle problems. Instead, show your child how to use healthy ways to cope with stress, such as exercising, listening to music, or talking your issues over with a friend.

COMMUNICATE NO TOLERANCE FOR SUBSTANCE USE

As a parent, you can have more influence over your child's behavior than his friends do, and more influence than music, TV, social networking sites, and celebrities. As mentioned previously, make it perfectly clear that you do not want your child to use tobacco, alcohol, or drugs. Period. Stress that it is unhealthy and it is illegal.

TALK WITH YOUR CHILDREN ABOUT DRUGS

Parents of very young children must quickly learn to answer a lot of questions—no matter how ridiculous they seem. Taking time to do so lets kids know that it's okay to ask questions and that you can be trusted to provide answers. Children don't forget this! As they grow, your own willingness to ask questions and to be a good listener is also important. It tells children you care about what

fashion, music, or movies they are interested in, and it provides you insight into their world.

These casual conversations don't have to be long and drawn out, but they are an excellent time to introduce the subject of drugs and alcohol. Don't worry that you are giving your child ideas. Kids are exposed to alcohol and drugs through the media every day. Even elementary school children likely know someone who uses prescription drugs for allergies or asthma. If not, they probably remember having a cold and being given medicine to make them feel better.

NOTE: *The following text suggests ways to talk with children at various ages. Although divided into preschool, elementary, middle school, and high school, the exact age range of students in these grade levels may be different in your area. Also, children don't necessarily develop at the same pace, and drug issues vary among communities. Use the suggestions most suitable to your child's maturity level and environment.*

Talking With Preschoolers

It may seem premature to talk about drugs with preschoolers, but the attitudes they form now are the foundation for the decisions they will make when they're older. Talk often with your preschoolers, and listen often to what they have to say.

1. **Playing grownup.** At this early age, children often like to play grownup by pretending to be adults. They mimic what adults do and say. What they hear you say and see you do makes a lasting impression, so when opportunities arise to let your child know how you feel about substance use, share those feelings. If you drive up to the supermarket, for example, and see someone standing outside smoking, tell your child that smoking is harmful and that it causes people to get very sick and sometimes die.

2. **Teaching on their level.** Children this age are capable of understanding your explanation

DOs AND DON'Ts OF TALKING WITH KIDS ABOUT DRUGS

When it comes to talking with kids at any age, make your messages clear and consistent.

DO:

- Tell them the dangers of using drugs and alcohol using **age-appropriate** explanations.

- Explain *why* you don't want them to use drugs. For example, explain how drugs and alcohol interfere with young people's concentration, memory, and motor skills, and that it leads to poorer school performance. Tell them you wouldn't want these outcomes for them.

- Make it easy for your child to talk honestly with you. Also, make yourself available when your child wants to talk—no matter the time of day or the other tasks you face.

- Believe in your own power to help your child avoid using alcohol and drugs.

DON'T:

- Don't react in anger—even if your child makes statements that shock you.

- Don't expect every conversation to be perfect. They won't be.

- Don't simply demand that your children not do drugs. Instead, educate them about the risks so they will be equipped to make decisions about drug use based on their own knowledge.

- Don't talk without listening. Aim for a 50/50 conversation—you talk half the time and listen the other half.

- Don't make stuff up. If your child asks a question you can't answer or wants information about something you're unsure of, promise to find the correct answer so you can learn together. Then follow up on that promise.

about poison and bad things in your home, such as cleaning products, paint, etc. Caution your children to eat or drink only what you, a grandparent, or another caregiver gives them. If your child becomes sick and you administer medicine, use this opportunity to explain that medicine helps the person it is meant for but can harm someone else who takes it. Warn children to never take a drug unless it is meant for them.

3. **Short but honest answers.** Preschool children are curious and eager to learn, but they also have relatively short attention spans.

When they ask questions, answer honestly but don't overwhelm them with information they aren't capable of understanding. For example, you or another adult family member occasionally drink wine with dinner or enjoy a beer on the weekend. Four-year-old Jimmy wants to know if he can taste it. You might say, *"No, Jimmy, this is only for adults who are at least 21 years old. It can make children very sick if they drink it. Why don't you help me fix you a glass of apple juice instead?"*

4. **Decisions, decisions ...** Even at this early stage of life, it's important to teach your children how to make good decisions. One way to do that is to let your children make their own decisions—but only if they don't endanger their well-being. For example:

> Explain early (and often) about why healthy foods help children grow up to be fit and strong. If they are especially enamored by a fictional character or famous athlete, encourage them to eat healthy foods so they will grow up to be healthy and strong like thier idols. This gives your child the background knowledge to make smart food choices.

> When feasible, let your pre-schooler choose what clothing to wear—even if they make a few mistakes. Letting them choose builds confidence in their own decision-making ability.

Talking With Elementary School Students (6–10 years old)

At the lower end of this age range, children are very perceptive and anxious to learn. This is a good time to introduce more detail into your conversations about drugs, especially what they are and the consequences of using them. Explain the concept of addiction—that some people may not understand how harmful drugs are or that some people try drugs and then have a hard time quitting. Introduce them to the idea that drug use can lead to abuse, which can lead to addiction.

1. **Good drugs and bad drugs.** Kids in this age group may ask why some drugs are good for you and others aren't. With the rise in prescription drug abuse, this is a good time to explain to them that prescription medication should be

taken only when a doctor tells you to and only when administered by an adult. Tell your child that bad drugs can make you sick or even kill you and that is why it is wrong to take them—even once. They may even understand the sadness that accompanies death if they've lost a loved one (such as a grandparent).

2. **Honesty and praise.** Explain in more detail how dangerous it is for children to drink alcohol and how harmful it is to their developing brain and body. Tell them the truth: even relatively small amounts of alcohol can make a child sick. If your children aspire to be like someone famous, such as a sports figure, remind them that it's important to take care of their body and not use tobacco, alcohol, or drugs if they want to excel. Children this age crave praise, so give it out freely when deserved. For example, let them know you think they are super smart for disliking the smell of cigarette smoke. This type of interaction also assures children they are capable of making healthy choices—in this case, they dislike cigarettes and don't want to be around them.

3. **Repeat yourself.** While in elementary school, children need to be warned about not using inhalants. (For a review, see the section on inhalants.) Tell them—repeatedly—that even one instance of inhaling can lead to severe brain damage or even death.

4. **When they ask ...** When children in this age group ask questions, it's often because of something they have seen or heard, and it's important to know where they are getting their information. For example, your eight-year-old may ask, *"What is pot?"* First, clarify that your child

Talk to your kids often about making good choices and about healthy living and smart goal setting.

CONVERSATION STARTERS

Starting a conversation about alcohol, tobacco, and other drugs with your kids is never easy—but it's also not as difficult as you may think. Take advantage of teachable moments to begin a conversation with your child when the opportunity arises.

- If you see a young person smoking a cigarette, you might talk about the negative effects of tobacco.

- If you see an interesting news story, discuss it with your child. Did a drunk driver hit and kill a family? Did a young couple lose custody of their children because they were busted for drugs? How does your child feel about what happened? What consequences does your child think are appropriate in these cases?

- While watching TV with your kids, ask them if they think the shows or the advertising make tobacco, alcohol, and drug use look cool? Do they change the way your child feels about drugs?

HOW ALCOHOL AND DRUGS ALTER BRAIN DEVELOPMENT AND FUNCTION

Most kids grow dramatically during the adolescent and teen years. Their young brains, particularly the *prefrontal cortex* that is used to make decisions, are growing and developing, too—even into their twenties! Alcohol can interfere with some of the developmental processes occurring in the brain. For weeks or months after a teen stops drinking heavily, parts of the brain still struggle to work correctly.[66] Drinking at a young age is also associated with the development of alcohol dependence later in life.

Long-term drug use causes brain changes that can set people up for addiction and other problems. Once young people become addicted, their brain becomes altered so that drugs are now their top priority—and they will compulsively seek and use drugs even though doing so brings devastating consequences for their lives and for those who care about them.

means marijuana by asking where your child learned about it and what exactly was heard, read, or seen. Based on that, you might answer, "*It's a very dangerous drug that people smoke—usually like a cigarette but sometimes in a pipe. Marijuana has chemicals in it that can cause cancer and maybe even kill you. People who smoke marijuana can get addicted and can't stop using it, or they might try other very dangerous drugs, too. It's nothing to mess around with, and I hope you don't ever try it. You are a smart girl, and I wouldn't want you to mess up your life.*"

5. **Involve others.** Children this age still respect adults, particularly law enforcement. As your child enters elementary school, offer to help establish or administer a drug education program that includes outside resources. For more information, review the resources in the back of this publication.

6. **Encourage healthy choices and smart decision-making.** Talk to your kids often about making good choices and about healthy living and smart goal setting. Let them make age-appropriate decisions, and reward them when they do well. Doing so empowers them and gives them confidence in their decision-making skills.

Talking With Middle School Students (11–14 years old)

Your child's transition to middle school (or junior high) calls for special vigilance. If you began having regular conversations with your child at a young age, the child should know by now—without a doubt—where you stand on the subject of drugs and alcohol. If you didn't have those conversations earlier,

it's not too late to start! In fact, this is the time when you should spend even *more* time talking and listening, as your child is likely seeing more substance use on television, in movies, and online—and at school or in social situations. Children this age are capable of engaging in more in-depth conversations about why people use drugs, the potential dangers (such as addiction or fatal overdose), and the consequences for the user and his family.

1. **Take the lead.** Your child may not initiate as many conversations about drugs and alcohol with you as before. If that's the case, it's important for you to take the lead and engage your child in discussions at every opportunity by using real-life events in the news or in your own lives. For example, your child tells you that a friend named Kevin rode in a vehicle driven by an older brother, who was smoking marijuana while driving. Explain to your child the importance of not riding in a car with someone who is using alcohol or drugs, and explain what to do in that situation. You might say, "*What Kevin's brother did was illegal, and he could go to jail if caught. But more important, he could have had a serious accident. I hope you know you can call me if that ever happens to you, and I will come and get you. You'll be driving in a few years, and I'm glad you are smart enough to know better than to drink or do drugs and drive.*"

2. **Encourage healthy growth.** Conversations with your child should also include talking about his interests. As discussed in the section on protective factors, activities such as youth groups, arts, music, sports, community service, and academic clubs keep

> Your ongoing conversations with your children should include how to respond if someone offers them drugs or alcohol. Let your child practice his answers.

children occupied, develop team-building skills, provide a sense of discipline, and sometimes help kids discover talents they didn't realize they had. Encourage your children to share their dreams—at the very least, ask what types of activities they enjoy, and then find a way to nurture those interests in positive ways.

3. **Self-image.** In this age range, preteens begin going through physical changes, and they start to care more about their self-image. Girls, especially, tend to pay more attention to hair and fashion. As you notice this happening, initiate conversations with your child about how he or she looks. Point out the obvious downsides to smoking, such as bad breath and stinky hair. You might even expand that into talking about the long-term risks, such as lung cancer and emphysema. For children who are interested in sports, encourage them to stay healthy and avoid anabolic steroids as a "quick fix" for enhancing their performance.

4. **Friends and their parents.** Friends become extremely important during this transition. Kids want to fit in or feel normal around older teens who may expose them to alcohol, tobacco, or drugs. So in addition to talking to your own child, get to know your children's friends. If you're

USE ROLE-PLAYING TO HELP YOUR CHILD SAY "NO" TO DRUGS

Encourage your children to analyze a situation and know how to remove themselves from a dangerous environment. A great way to prepare your children for real-life situations is to act out scenarios with them so that they can practice how they'll respond. Use the following two scenarios as a starting point, and create new ones based on your child's age and activities.

Scenario #1: Your child goes to a party at a friend's house and someone has brought some beer. Many of the guys there, including older high school guys, are drinking and they ask your child, "You want some?" Take the role of the older teens or of your child's friends who casually offer a can of beer to your child.

Help your child develop firm but friendly responses. Possible answers:

- "No, thanks."
- "No, I'm not into that."
- "Nah man, I'm ok. Thanks."
- "No, thanks. I'm on the _____ team and I don't want to risk it."
- "Nah, I'm training for _____."
- "No. I gotta go in a bit."

Scenario #2: Your child is at a friend's house with a few close pals and one of them pulls out a joint. While you play the role of the friend offering it to the group, help your child develop firm but friendly responses, and reassure your child that good friends will respect the decision not to try it. Possible answers:

- "No, thanks, I'm not into that."
- "No, thanks. I'm on the _____ team and I don't want to risk it."
- "Nah, I'm training for _____."
- "Nah. I get tested at work/school and I don't want to risk it."
- "No, thanks. I don't like how it makes people act."
- "No, I'm trying to stay healthy for _____."

If your child's peers keep insisting, suggest that your child use the "broken record" technique—just keep repeating the reason for not wanting to drink, smoke, or do drugs. Then your child can try to change the subject or, if all else fails, your child can simply go home.

giving a group of kids a ride to the mall, for example, make small talk with the friends by asking about their interests, their family, what music or television shows they like, etc. And as discussed earlier in this publication, get to know the parents of your child's friends and share with them your desire to raise a drug-free child. You may find some who do not share your attitude and beliefs about drugs and underage alcohol use. But think of it this way: if they *do* agree and your child regularly hangs out with the same five friends, you could have as many as 10 extra parents keeping their eyes and ears on your child's activities!

DANGERS OF UNDERAGE DRINKING[67]

- Alcohol impairs coordination, slows reaction time, and impairs vision.

- Beer and wine are not "safer" than hard liquor. A 12-ounce can of beer, a 5-ounce glass of wine, and 1.5 ounces of hard liquor all contain the same amount of alcohol and have the same effects on the body and mind.

- On average, it takes 2–3 hours for a single drink to leave a person's system. Nothing can speed up this process, including drinking coffee, taking a cold shower, or walking it off.

- People tend to be very bad at judging how seriously alcohol has affected them. That means many individuals who drive after drinking think they can control a car—but they actually cannot.

- Anyone can develop a serious alcohol problem, including a teenager. This is especially true if there is a family history of alcoholism.

- Underage drinking is illegal, and getting caught may mean trouble with the authorities.

- Drinking may cause people to engage in risky behavior they normally wouldn't have.

5. **Practice makes perfect.** Your ongoing conversations with your children should include how to respond if someone offers them drugs or alcohol. Let your child practice his answers. *"Man, that stuff is really bad for you!"* or *"My mom will kill me if she finds out I drank a beer!"* As mentioned earlier in this publication, assure your children you will come get them any time—without scolding—if they need to leave a place where alcohol or drugs are being used. If you can't be available, find a responsible adult who will go in your place.

6. **Asking and listening.** Remember, your role as a parent (or caregiver) isn't just to talk but also to listen. Since your child may not ask as many questions at this age, it's up to **YOU** to ask open-ended questions that require more than a simple "yes" or "no" answer. Conversation starters can come from the media (advertising, song lyrics, movies, TV shows) or from real life. For example, you might say

   › In that movie last night, the character continued to drink even after she found out she was pregnant. How do you think that might affect her unborn baby?

   › My coworker Mary has a 14-year-old child who got busted for pot and will have to go into a substance abuse treatment center. What do you think that will be like?

7. **Your role as a teacher.** You must also take the role of an educator. For example, young teens may think it's okay if they "only" drink but stay away from drugs. You need to tell them the real risks of all kinds of substance abuse—including the risks they may not have heard or thought about—or teach them how to find credible information on websites like **www.justthinktwice.com**, which was developed for teens and young adults.

8. **A particular concern.** Just as with elementary school students, the use of inhalants is of particular concern at this age. In a 2011 survey, 7 percent of eighth-graders reported using inhalants in the year prior to the survey, and 39 percent of eighth-graders didn't consider the regular use of inhalants to be harmful.[68] This is troubling because inhalants can cause unconsciousness, severe damage to the brain and nervous system, and even death—the first time they are used! Yet 64 percent of the eighth-graders surveyed didn't think trying inhalants once or twice was risky. Young teens may not understand the risks of inhalant use, so it's up to you to educate them about the dangers.

9. **What do *they* think?** Continue to teach your children to be critical of how drugs and alcohol are portrayed in videos, movies, and television shows. Do they think engaging in promiscuous behavior after drinking too much is attractive or disgusting? Does a video that shows drugs make them curious enough to want to try them? Continue to talk to your kids often about making good choices and about healthy living and goal setting.

Talking With High School Students (15–18 years old)

By the time teens enter high school, they have likely had many opportunities to try drugs, alcohol, and/or tobacco. Even if they have resisted the temptation, they've probably seen their peers do it—sometimes to excess and perhaps even with serious consequences. In fact, they may know fellow classmates with addiction issues. You can't choose your children's friends—although parents have been trying for years! But you *can* encourage them to develop friendships with kids who do not smoke, drink, or do drugs.

1. **What they're thinking.** Teens this age typically understand how substance use can affect unborn

children, how combining drugs can be deadly, and how easy it is to go from casual use to abuse to addiction. Enforce these concepts when talking with your teenager. During the last few years of high school, teens are thinking about what their future holds, so this is a great time to keep reminding them that substance use can ruin their chances of getting into college, being accepted by the military, or being hired for certain jobs. Also, remind them that keeping the community drug free will make it a nicer place to raise a family if they decide to put down roots there.

2. **Debating what's legal.** An important issue to discuss with your teenager (**and** with your preteen in middle school) is the debate over medical marijuana. Make sure your child knows that "smoked marijuana" has **not** withstood the rigors of science—it is **not** medicine and it is **not** safe. Marijuana **is** harmful and it **is** illegal.

3. **Granting independence—with love.** Children this age want independence, but you need to set limits. Set curfews and other expectations for your child's behavior, establish appropriate consequences for breaking rules, and consistently follow through with enforcement. Finally, tell children often that you care about them and that they are important to you. *Show* them you mean it by regularly spending one-on-one time with them. Developing this strong bond will make your child more likely to come to you with questions or concerns about drugs, alcohol, or other sensitive issues—encourage that openness. Remember, even as children are pushing for independence, they need someone they love and respect to be involved. They need **YOU**!

4. **Know what's trendy.** Talk with your teen about what you learn here and elsewhere about the dangers of abusing prescription drugs. Non-medical use of prescription medications to get high is rising dramatically, as shown in the section on prescription medications. The **Drug Identification Chart** at the back of this publication is a good way to help you identify some prescription drugs, but other medications become trendy at times, and other drugs may be specific to your community that aren't shown in the chart. Routinely ask your teen which prescription drugs are an issue at school, in friends' homes, and at parties.

5. **Drinking or drug use while driving.** As teens begin to drive and become even more independent, establish clear rules about drinking or using drugs while driving. Ask for their input; then develop a written agreement that spells out expectations for behavior and specific consequences for breaking the rules. For example, you may want to limit the hours your teen can drive and grant (or deny) permission to transport younger siblings. Whether or not your city or state restricts the number of passengers in your teen's car, you can do so as part of your written agreement. You and your young driver should sign the agreement to give it more credibility, then keep it in a public area of the home to serve as a constant reminder of what is expected. Here are a few other examples you might include.

> I will not drink alcohol and drive.

> I will drive only from ____

MARIJUANA MYTHS

Myth: Marijuana is not harmful because it is all natural and comes from a plant.

Truth: Tobacco comes from a plant, too—but that hardly makes it safe. Both contain cancer-causing compounds. Smoking anything is not good for the lungs.

Myth: It's okay to use marijuana as long as you're not a chronic user or "stoner."

Truth: You can't predict when occasional use will turn into frequent use, problematic use, or addiction—and even occasional users can get into car wrecks or other accidents while under the influence of marijuana.

Myth: Marijuana isn't as bad as other drugs, and I doubt I'd get in trouble if I get caught.

Truth: Marijuana can be as bad as other drugs—it affects your memory, mood, and coordination. It is addictive, and it is illegal!

or at least be familiar with the name of the person who is responsible for campus counseling or prevention programs.

Learn about the college's standards of conduct. Federal regulations require any institution of higher education receiving federal funding (most of them do) to have a drug prevention program that prohibits, at a minimum, the unlawful possession, use, or distribution of illicit drugs and alcohol by students on campus property or while participating in its activities. Colleges must enforce these standards or risk serious consequences, including loss of federal student financial assistance. Ask about and understand the college's parental notification policy for standards of conduct violations. Make sure your child understands the penalties for underage drinking, public drunkenness, illicit drug use, using a fake ID, driving under the influence of drugs or alcohol, assault, and other alcohol-related offenses.

Make certain your child understands how alcohol and other illicit drug use and abuse can be associated with date rape, violence, and academic failure, as well as have consequences after graduation.

This is also an important time to stress the importance of the responsible consumption of alcohol when your college-age children are of legal drinking age, and if they choose to drink.

> I will not stay at a party where alcohol is served or drugs are present.

> I will not ride in a car with a driver who has been drinking or using drugs.

6. **The "at home" party.** Some parents mistakenly believe *"My teens and their friends are safer drinking at home because they aren't out driving while intoxicated."* Even if state law permits teens to drink at home at certain ages under a parent's supervision, it doesn't mean you should let them. Doing so may be setting a dangerous example—essentially signaling you approve of what may be illegal consumption of alcohol in other settings. And if you give your teen permission to host a party in your home, never supply alcohol to your child's friends. Not only is it illegal, but you may well be held liable for anything that happens to the minors and any damage they cause— including what happens when they leave the premises. Make sure two responsible adults are present to monitor the festivities in your home.

7. **Continue to praise and encourage teenagers for the things they do well and the positive choices they make.** Knowing you are proud of them can motivate them to maintain a drug-free lifestyle and to serve as a positive role model for younger siblings.

Parenting doesn't stop when a child goes to college.[69]

Find out if there is a program during freshman orientation that educates students about campus policies, and health and wellness or prevention programs related to alcohol and other drug use. If so, attend with your child,

63 *Monitoring the Future national survey results on drug use, 1975–2010: Volume I, Secondary school students. Overview of Key Findings*

64 National Institute on Drug Abuse. *Preventing Drug Abuse among Children and Adolescents (In Brief). How can the community develop a plan for research-based prevention?* NIH Publication No. 04-4212(B). 1997. Updated October 2003.

65 Centers for Disease Control and Prevention. *Parent Engagement: Strategies for Involving Parents in School Health.* 2012. Accessed September 21, 2012, **www.cdc.gov/healthyyouth/adolescenthealth/pdf/parent_engagement_factsheet.pdf**.

66 National Institute on Drug Abuse. NIDA for Teens, The Science Behind Drugs Abuse: The Sara Bellum Blog. *Real Teens Ask: Got Alcohol on the Brain?* Posted May 24, 2011. Accessed September 21, 2012, **http://teens.drugabuse.gov/blog/real-teens-ask-alcohol-brain**.

67 *Make a Difference – Talk To Your Child About Alcohol.*

68 *Monitoring the Future national results on adolescent drug use: Overview of key findings, 2011.*

69 National Institute on Alcohol Abuse and Alcoholism. *What Parents Need to Know About College Drinking.* NIH Publication No. 02-5015. Printed April 2002. Accessed September 21, 2012, **www.collegedrinkingprevention.gov/media/FINALParents.pdf**.

Sometimes—despite the best efforts of parents—kids still experiment with drugs or alcohol. And sometimes experimentation leads to abuse and/or addiction.

SIGNS OF ABUSE

What if you suspect your child is using alcohol or drugs? First, realize that some signs that *might* indicate a problem with alcohol or drugs can simply be normal teenage behavior—but that doesn't mean you should ignore them. When you're trying to figure out what your teen has been up to, it makes sense to make use of all of your senses.[70]

> **Sight:** Take a look at your teen. Red eyes and cheeks, or difficulty focusing on you, may indicate your teen has been drinking alcohol. Red eyes and constricted pupils can be a sign of marijuana use. A strange burn on the mouth or fingers of your child can be a sign of smoking something through a metal or glass pipe. Someone wearing long sleeves in the middle of the summer may be trying to hide puncture marks that would indicate intravenous drug use. Chronic nosebleeds may be a sign of cocaine abuse.

> **Smell:** Marijuana, cigarettes, and alcohol all have very telltale smells. And whether you notice them on your teen's breath or on clothing, they are reason for alarm—simply being around other teens who may be drinking or smoking makes it more likely that your teen will too. Follow your nose—and don't forget that excessive "good" smells, like breath fresheners, heavy perfumes, and freshly laundered clothing (especially for a teen who's never run the washing machine) can be as telling as the smells they're trying to mask. And make sure that you take a whiff of your teen's car—the smell of stale beer or marijuana smoke may linger in the car's upholstery.

> **Sound:** Listen for the clues that teens give you by the things they say, the things they laugh at, or the fact that they aren't saying anything at all. Silence can speak volumes about the fact that something's going on in your teen's life. By continuing to listen over time, you'll be able to identify which behaviors are the result of a short-term mood swing and which are indicative of a more serious underlying issue.

Is there a potentially rational explanation for many of these scenarios? Certainly—your teen may be suffering from a cold, trying to mask eczema on the arms, may just be tired, may be feeling stressed by a difficult class in school, or may

When it comes to identifying the signs of drug abuse, the best rule to follow is this: No one knows your kids better than you. If you think something's going on, take the steps necessary to find out for certain.

be having issues in a relationship. By observing your teen using all of your senses, combined with your gut instinct, you'll be better able to determine if a certain behavior is "typical" or indicative of drug use.

Other signs to look for that may indicate drug use include

> Stories don't add up, and social circles change. When your teen goes to the football game but can't tell you which team won, or tells you about staying at a friend's house but the friend called your house asking to speak to your teen, it's time to be concerned. No matter how much your teen denies there's anything going on, it's up to you to confront your child and get to the heart of the issue. The same thing holds true if you see a sudden change in your child's social circle. If your teen is no longer associating with childhood friends, seems to be interested in hanging out with kids who are older, or is simply spending time with new friends that give you a bad feeling, you should follow your instincts. And don't accept sullen silence as an answer—make sure the conversation occurs.

> School goes downhill. Declining grades can be a stark indicator

that drug abuse is occurring—especially if your teen typically performs well. A loss of motivation, missing homework, skipping school, or foregoing extracurricular activities may be signs that there is a drug issue.

> Lying and stealing. Your six-pack of beer has suddenly turned into a five-pack. Your after-dinner aperitif tastes suspiciously watered-down. You're missing cash from your wallet or a gold ring from your jewelry box. When teens want to get drunk or high, one of the first places they're going to go looking for "resources" is within their own homes. If you begin to notice missing items, you must immediately confront your child with your suspicions and say that stealing—whether it be $5 from your purse or a $500 necklace—will not be tolerated.

When it comes to identifying the signs of drug abuse, the best rule to follow is this: No one knows your kids better than you. If you think something's going on, take the steps necessary to find out for certain.

IS IT OKAY TO SNOOP?

Sometimes parents who suspect their child is using drugs wonder whether it is okay to snoop. Only *you* can decide that, but keep in mind that you are suspicious for a reason—and your suspicions may be right. Remember, it is **your** house, and **you** are the parent. And if you have young children in the home, you certainly wouldn't want them to find something harmful.

Where would you look? And for what? Well, drugs are easily hidden in drawers, backpacks, the back of closets, the corners of bed sheets, small boxes, books or bookcases, makeup cases, over-the-counter medicine bottles, and under the mattresses or beds. You might also find drug *paraphernalia*

(items related to drug use), such as pipes, rolling papers, medicine bottles, eye drops, butane lighters, or homemade pipes and *bongs* (pipes that use water as a filter) made from soda cans or plastic beverage containers. If you suspect your child is drinking, look for empty cans or bottles.

HOW TO PROCEED

Maybe you found evidence. Maybe not. But even if all you have are suspicions, you need to take action. Remember the section on myths. Denying a problem exists does not mean there isn't one, and ignoring signs of trouble won't make a problem go away.

NOTE: Many of the recommendations in this section were adapted from

> **http://timetoact.drugfree.org** and

> **www.getsmartaboutdrugs. com/help/intervene.html**

More tips and videos are available on those websites.

> If you have a partner or spouse, tell him or her about your suspicions and plan your actions together. If you're a single parent, you may want to speak with someone else, such as a doctor, psychologist, pastoral advisor, school nurse, and/or a school drug and alcohol counselor. Use the person as a sounding board of sorts—someone unbiased who can help you sort out your feelings.

> Before talking with your child, practice the conversation until you are sure you can remain calm. Also, don't initiate the conversation unless you're sure your child is sober or has not been using drugs, which may mean waiting until the next day.

> What do you say? Begin by voicing your suspicions without making accusations. *"Susan, I suspect you may be smoking pot occasionally. I love you and I'm concerned about you. Is there something going on that we need to talk about?"*

> Be prepared emotionally for possible reactions. Your child may accuse you of snooping. Your child may tell you that you're crazy or call you a hypocrite (especially if you smoke or occasionally have a drink). Your child may express hatred and threaten to leave home.

> Whatever the response, make your mind up ahead of time to remain calm. Even if your child denies there is a problem (which will probably happen), reinforce what you believe about drugs and how much you care about your child. *"I want to believe you, sweetheart, because there is a lot of evidence that young people who use drugs are at risk for many bad things. I'd be very disappointed if you didn't finish school or if someone took advantage of you sexually while you were high."*

> Having this type of calm, open discussion at least lets your children know you care and that you still love them. Follow up by being a parent. *"And remember, we had a deal that no member of this family would use drugs."* Enforce whatever discipline you agreed on for breaking the rules (if that is the case).

> During this conversation, it's very important for your child to feel supported, so continue to remind your child that you're always there for guidance, especially during a stressful time when your child may be tempted to use. Express your love, care, and concern to your child—both in your words and in your tone. *"Sweetheart, I*

MEET GARRETT HARNEY

Cindy Harney beams with pride as she speaks about her son Garrett.

"Garrett loved to play the piano. He loved all kinds of sports—he wake boarded, skate boarded, and played in Little League. He also cared about the community. He loved 4-H and was on the board of a local organization for children with learning disabilities. Everyone here knew him by his F-150 pickup. But after a friend shared his mother's pain medicine, Garrett's life was never the same. Nor was ours."

Garrett died at the age of 20 from a prescription drug overdose of Oxycodone and Xanax. In addition to his parents, Garrett left behind a sister just 16 months younger than he was—a sister who now has no sibling with whom to share her life experiences.

"There isn't a day goes by that I don't think of my boy," says Cindy. "I told him about all the illicit drugs, but I never told him about legal drugs. No parent should ever have to pick out the casket for their child or the clothes he will wear to be buried in."

Determined not to let her son die in vain, Cindy now shares her horrific experience to help educate others—parents, youths, law enforcement, the medical community, and lawmakers—about the dangers of prescription drug abuse in hopes of enacting change.

"After Garrett's death, I learned that many kids in my Florida community were dying because of prescription drugs, and I knew I had to do something. I met a woman whose 18-year-old son had taken his life and asked her if she would join me in the fight against drug abuse. We traveled to Kentucky to learn about its prescription drug monitoring program, and then we went to Tallahassee in hopes of getting a similar program in Florida."

Cindy and her new acquaintance also founded Families Against Addictive Drug Abuse to create awareness of the problem and to enact change. She played a role in the creation of a prescription drug task force in her local sheriff's department and in the development of Operation Medicine Cabinet, a countywide project to take back old medicine. She also speaks at local, regional, and national events.

"We're losing approximately 10 Floridians a day, and that's more than by all illegal drugs combined. We must take action so no other family has to suffer the loss that we have. Hopefully, through education and by working together as a community, we'll be able to educate our little ones so they never fall into this epidemic."

Currently, Cindy Harney is working with Florida Congressman Vernon Buchanan's office to get support for the Pill Mill Crackdown Bill (H.R. 1065) to increase penalties for the operators of pill mills. (A pill mill is a facility that violates federal or state laws that pertain to prescribing and dispensing controlled substances.)

Garrett Harney and his sister

want to discuss this because I love and care about you, and I want you to be healthy, safe, and successful."

A word of caution. It's human nature to want to believe your children when they say they aren't using drugs. They may say they are stashing a pipe for someone else or tired because of extra schoolwork, or they may provide any number of excuses that sound rational. But if your suspicions are strong—and especially if you are faced with hard evidence—do not pretend that everything is fine. It obviously isn't. Also, do not blame yourself. Drug abuse occurs in all kinds of families.

If the conversation becomes heated or out of control, don't continue. Assure your child you love him or her and end the discussion peacefully. You've at least taken a big step, and you can always try again another day.

If your child flatly refuses to talk to you about it, ask for help from a school guidance counselor, family physician, or a local drug treatment referral and assessment center. Your child's school may even have a counselor qualified to evaluate your child and refer you to a particular agency for treatment.

ADDICTION

No one plans to become addicted. Instead, it begins with a single use, which can lead to abuse, which can lead to addiction—a disease in which a person craves the drug (or alcohol or nicotine) regardless of the consequences. Remember, however, that children with more risk factors may be more susceptible to using and becoming addicted.

For many years, society believed that people addicted to drugs lacked willpower or were morally flawed. Today, the National Institute on Drug Abuse (NIDA) defines addiction as "a chronic, relapsing brain disease that is characterized by compulsive drug seeking and use, despite harmful consequences. It is considered a brain disease because drugs change the brain—they change its structure and how it works. These brain changes can be long lasting and can lead to the harmful behaviors seen in people who abuse drugs."

The good news is that addiction is a treatable disease, but the success of any treatment approach depends on a variety of factors, including a child's temperament and willingness to change. It may take several attempts before a child remains drug free, so do not give up hope. You are not alone!

FINDING TREATMENT

When your child is referred for treatment, it's important to find a program best suited to your child's needs.

> Your first step in this journey is to find a certified drug and alcohol counselor. To do that, consult your child's doctor, other parents whose children have been treated for drug abuse, the local hospital, a school social worker, the school district's substance abuse coordinator, or the county mental health society.

> Or, you may call the U.S. Department of Health and Human Services Substance Abuse and Mental Health Services Administration (SAMHSA) toll-free at 1-800-662-HELP (4357) for alcohol and drug information and treatment referral assistance. When you call this toll-free number, a recorded message gives you the option to speak to a representative concerning substance abuse treatment, or to request printed material on alcohol or drugs.

> Online, parents can go to the Partnership At Drugfree.org (**www.drugfree.org**), a nonprofit organization that helps parents

and caregivers prevent, intervene in, and find treatment for drug and alcohol use by their children.

> At **www.findtreatment.samhsa. gov**, you'll find more than 11,000 addiction treatment programs, including residential treatment centers, outpatient treatment programs, and hospital inpatient programs for drug addiction and alcoholism. Listings include treatment programs for marijuana, cocaine, and heroin addiction, as well as drug and alcohol treatment programs for adolescents and adults.

> Another drug and alcohol addiction treatment website is **www.drugstrategies.org**, which is dedicated to providing local resources for fighting substance abuse. It also offers a 24-hour hotline at 1-800-559-9503. Also, check the resources at the back of this publication for other possibilities.

RECOVERY

Addiction is typically a chronic disease, so people cannot simply stop using drugs for a few days and be cured. Relapse is not uncommon. Most patients require long-term or repeated episodes of care to achieve sustained abstinence and recovery.

Because the risk of relapse is highest for youths in the time period directly following treatment, the transition to the school setting is an important time when appropriate relapse prevention services could increase the likelihood of long-term recovery.[71]

Families will need to access recovery support services for their child to help successfully navigate the early months of recovery. Some of these services will provide a flexible and cost-effective mechanism for facilitating access to services.

Some recovery services already exist within the education community, including recovery schools. Recovery high schools provide a service-enriched and supportive school environment for students recovering from drug and alcohol problems. They offer standard academic courses, combined with continuing care and/or recovery support services, but they generally do not provide substance use or mental health disorder treatment. The Association of Recovery Schools (ARS) website at **www.recoveryschools.org** provides additional information and includes a list of recovery high schools.

Don't be surprised if—somewhere during the process of getting treatment for your child—a suggestion is made that the entire family get counseling, too. Treating addiction isn't simply about healing the abuser. Some parents become so obsessed with their child's problem that they neglect the other important aspects of their own lives: their jobs, physical health, and other kids. It is as important to seek help for your own emotional well-being as it is for the child using drugs. Every member of the family needs to be committed to helping the recovering addict stay clean and sober.

---

[70] Drug Enforcement Administration. *Get Smart About Drugs. A DEA Resource for Parents*. Signs of Drug Use: Behavior. Accessed September 21, 2012, **www.getsmartaboutdrugs.com/identify/behavior.html**.

[71] U.S. Department of Education, Office of Safe and Drug-Free Schools. *Recovery/Relapse Prevention in Educational Settings for Youth with Substance Use and Co-occurring Mental Health Disorders*. 2010 Consultative Sessions. Working Draft May 2011. Accessed September 21, 2012, **www2.ed.gov/about/offices/list/osdfs/recoveryrpt.pdf**.

NOTE: *We don't endorse any private or commercial products or services that are not affiliated with the federal government, and the sources of information on these pages are intended only as a partial listing. Readers of this booklet are encouraged to research and inform themselves of the many additional products and services relating to tobacco, drug, and alcohol abuse.*

PARENTS: Some websites kids go to for information about drugs or alcohol are sponsored by organizations with a hidden agenda, such as trying to get drugs legalized or decriminalized. Encourage your children to visit the following websites instead for credible information about tobacco, drugs, and alcohol.

FOR YOUTHS

AboveTheInfluence.com
www.abovetheinfluence.com

This campaign is inspired by what teens say about their lives and how they deal with the influences that shape their decisions about not using drugs or alcohol. The goal is to help teens stand up to negative pressures or influences.

Al-Anon Family Groups – Alateens
www.al-anon.alateen.org/for-alateen

Alateen is part of the Al-Anon Family Groups. Al-Anon is for anyone affected by someone else's drinking. *This link is to the section of the Al-Anon website specifically for teens.*

American Council for Drug Education (ACDE)
www.acde.org/youth

ACDE is an agency that develops substance abuse prevention and education programs and materials. *This link is to the section of their website specifically for youths* who are involved (or want to be involved) in a community coalition or who are passionate about keeping their communities safe and drug free.

D.A.R.E – Drug Abuse Resistance Education
www.dare.com/kids

D.A.R.E.'s primary mission is to provide children with the information and skills they need to live drug- and violence-free lives. *This link is to the section of their website specifically for youths.*

JustThinkTwice.com
www.justthinktwice.com

Created by the Drug Enforcement Administration (DEA) specifically for young people, this site provides information about drugs and their consequences.

National Suicide Prevention Lifeline
www.suicidepreventionlifeline.org

This crisis hotline can help with a lot of issues, not just suicide. For example, anyone who feels sad, hopeless, or suicidal; family and friends who are concerned about a loved one; victims of bullying; or anyone who is interested in mental health treatment referrals can call 1-800-273-TALK (8255). Callers are connected with a professional who will talk with them about what they're feeling or about concerns for other family and friends. The hotline is funded by the Substance Abuse and Mental Health Services Administration.

NIDA for Teens
http://teens.drugabuse.gov

The National Institute on Drug Abuse (NIDA) developed this website. Teens can get facts about drugs and drug effects, read advice from fellow teens, watch educational videos, download cool anti-drug material, and try their hand at brain games.

TheCoolSpot.gov
www.thecoolspot.gov

The Cool Spot was created by the National Institute on Alcohol Abuse and Alcoholism for kids 11–13 years old. Content is based on a curriculum for grades 6–8 developed by the University of Michigan to give young teens a clearer picture about alcohol use among their peers. The Cool Spot also features quizzes, tips for handling peer pressure, and links to educational and support sites.

FOR PARENTS

Depending on the age and maturity level of your children, you may wish to share some of the links in this section with them.

African American Family Services (AAFS)
www.aafs.net

AAFS works with individuals, families, and communities impacted by addiction and mental illness. They provide culturally specific chemical and mental health services that affect family preservation and promote community-based change and wellness in the African-American community.

Alcoholics Anonymous (AA)
www.aa.org

Alcoholics Anonymous is a fellowship of men and women who share their experience, strength, and hope with each other so they may solve their common problems and help others recover from alcoholism. The only requirement for membership is a desire to stop drinking. There are no dues or fees, and AA is not allied with any sect, denomination, politics, organization, or institution.

Al-Anon Family Groups
www.al-anon.org

Al-Anon is a free, nonprofit organization that supports and provides literature to family members and friends of alcoholics.

American Cancer Society
www.cancer.org

The American Cancer Society offers literature on smoking and referrals to local chapters.

American Council for Drug Education (ACDE)
www.acde.org

ACDE has educational programs and services designed to engage teens, address the needs of parents, and provide employers, educators, health professionals, policymakers, and the media with authoritative information on tobacco, alcohol, and other drugs.

Association of Recovery Schools (ARS)
www.recoveryschools.org

The Association of Recovery Schools advocates for the promotion, strengthening, and expansion of secondary and postsecondary programs designed for students and families committed to achieving success in both education and recovery. ARS exists to support such schools which, as components of the recovery continuum of care, enroll students committed to being abstinent from alcohol and other drugs and working a program of recovery.

Boys & Girls Clubs of America (BGCA)
www.bgca.org

The mission of Boys & Girls Clubs of America is to enable all young people to reach their full potential as productive, caring, responsible citizens.

College Drinking Prevention – Changing the Culture
www.collegedrinkingprevention.gov

This National Institute on Alcohol Abuse and Alcoholism site contains a wealth of information for parents, students, and educators about alcohol use on U.S. college campuses.

Community Anti-Drug Coalitions of America (CADCA)
www.cadca.org

CADCA is an organization whose purpose is to strengthen the capacity of community anti-drug coalitions to create and maintain safe, healthy, and drug-free communities.

D.A.R.E. – Drug Abuse Resistance Education
www.dare.com

D.A.R.E.'s primary mission is to provide children with the information and skills they need to live drug- and violence-free lives.

United States Drug Enforcement Administration (DEA)
www.justice.gov/dea

The mission of the DEA is to enforce the controlled substances laws and regulations of the United States and to recommend and support non-enforcement programs aimed at reducing the availability of illicit controlled substances on the domestic and international markets. The DEA has created a drug education website for teens at **www.justthinktwice.com** and a drug education resource for parents at **www.getsmartaboutdrugs.com**.

DrugStrategies.org
www.drugstrategies.org

This is a drug and alcohol addiction treatment website dedicated to providing resources for fighting substance abuse, including helping you find drug treatment centers and addiction rehabilitation programs in your town or city. The toll-free 24-hour hotline number is 1-800-559-9503.

Easy-to-Read Drug Facts

www.easyread.drugabuse.gov

Created by the National Institute on Drug Abuse, this easy-to-read website talks about drug abuse, addiction, and treatment. It has pictures and videos to help readers understand the text and can also read each page out loud. The pages are easy to print out to share with people who do not have computers.

Elks Drug Awareness Program

www.elks.org

The Benevolent and Protective Order of Elks has a resource center for the *Elks National Drug Awareness Program*, the largest volunteer drug awareness program in the United States. It provides information for parents and a guide for teachers, as well as educational comics for fourth- through eighth-graders, tips for teens, and contests.

Families Anonymous, Inc.

www.familiesanonymous.org

This organization is a 12-step fellowship for families and friends who have known a feeling of desperation concerning the destructive behavior of someone very near to them, whether caused by drugs, alcohol, or related behavioral problems.

GetSmartAboutDrugs

www.getsmartaboutdrugs.com

Created by the Drug Enforcement Administration (DEA) for parents, this website provides valuable drug education and prevention resources for parents. Information includes how to identify drugs and tips to help prevent drug abuse.

Higher Education Center for Alcohol, Drug Abuse, and Violence Prevention

http://higheredcenter.ed.gov

Created by the U.S. Department of Education, this site supports institutions of higher education in their efforts to prevent illegal alcohol and other drug use and its consequences, including violence, at U.S. colleges and universities.

Mothers Against Drunk Driving (MADD)

www.madd.org

Originally founded to combat drunk driving, this organization's current mission is also to support victims of this violent crime and to prevent underage drinking.

Narcotics Anonymous

www.na.org

Narcotics Anonymous is a 12-step fellowship of recovering addicts. Membership is open to all drug addicts, regardless of the particular drug or combination of drugs used. Meetings are free.

Nar-Anon

www.nar-anon.org

Nar-Anon is a 12-step program designed to help relatives and friends of addicts recover from the effects of living with an addicted relative or friend.

National Association for Children of Alcoholics (NACOA)

www.nacoa.org

NACOA's mission is to eliminate the adverse impact of alcohol and drug use on children and families.

National Association of School Nurses
www.nasn.org

The National Association of School Nurses improves the health and academic success of students by developing and providing leadership to advance the school nursing practice by specialized registered nurses. The organization's core purpose is to promote student success through the advancement of school health services by professional registered school nurses.

National Council on Alcoholism and Drug Dependence, Inc.
www.ncadd.org

An organization that provides information on how to overcome alcohol and drug addiction, including how to find help in your area.

National Crime Prevention Council (NCPC)
www.ncpc.org

A private nonprofit organization whose mission is to help families and their communities keep safe from crime, including on the Internet.

National Guard Counterdrug Program
http://ngbcounterdrug.ng.mil

The National Guard Counterdrug Program uses National Guard resources to help create the best opportunity for America's youths to make the decision to be drug free. They work with local law enforcement, education and community-based organizations to reduce the chances of exposure of illegal drugs to our nation's children.

National Inhalant Prevention Coalition (NIPC)
www.inhalants.org

NIPC serves as an inhalant referral and information clearinghouse, stimulates media coverage about inhalant issues, develops materials, and provides training and technical assistance.

National Institute on Alcohol Abuse and Alcoholism (NIAAA)
www.niaaa.nih.gov

The NIAAA website offers pamphlets, fact sheets, and brochures about alcohol-related problems such as underage drinking, alcohol's impact on health, parenting to prevent childhood alcohol use, and much more. For information on alcohol policy, go to **www.alcoholpolicy.niaaa.nih.gov**. For statistics and the latest news on stopping underage drinking, go to **https://stopalcoholabuse.gov**.

National Institute on Drug Abuse (NIDA)
www.nida.nih.gov

NIDA's mission is to lead the nation in bringing the power of science to bear on drug abuse and addiction through (1) support and conduct of research, and (2) quick dissemination of research results. The website features a section for parents and teachers, as well as a section for students and young adults. NIDA provides educational materials can be downloaded or ordered at **http://drugpubs.drugabuse.gov**.

National Suicide Prevention Lifeline
www.suicidepreventionlifeline.org

This crisis hotline can help with a lot of issues, not just suicide. For example, anyone who feels sad, hopeless, or suicidal; family and friends who are concerned about a loved one; victims of bullying; or anyone who is interested in mental health treatment referrals can call 1-800-273-TALK (8255). Callers are connected with a professional who will talk with them about what they're feeling or about concerns for other family and friends. The hotline is funded by the Substance Abuse and Mental Health Services Administration.

Office of National Drug Control (ONDCP)
www.whitehouse.gov/ondcp

ONDCP advises the president on U.S. drug-control issues, coordinates drug-control activities and related funding across the federal government, and produces the annual National Drug Control Strategy, which outlines administration efforts to reduce illicit drug use, manufacturing and trafficking, drug-related crime and violence, and drug-related health consequences.

PartnershipAtDrugFree.org (PDFA)
www.drugfree.org

PDFA is a nonprofit organization that helps parents and caregivers prevent, intervene in, and find treatment for drug and alcohol use by their children. PDFA also maintains the Parents Toll-Free Helpline (in English or Spanish) at 1-855-DRUGFREE (1-855-378-4373).

PreventTeenDrugUse.org
www.preventteendruguse.org

This organization provides parents with relevant research on marijuana and other drug use. It outlines the serious long-term negative effects drug use can have on youths, including lower academic achievement, school dropout rates, mental health problems, and addiction. Personal stories from a teen, a father, and a physician demonstrate how drug use can adversely affect youths, families, and communities. The website features videos reviewing current information and identifies prevention and treatment resources.

StopAlcoholAbuse.Gov
www.stopsalcoholabuse.gov

A parent's gateway to comprehensive research and resources on the prevention of underage drinking. Materials available through this portal are provided by the 15 Federal agencies of the Interagency Coordinating Committee on the Prevention of Underage Drinking.

Students against Destructive Decisions (SADD)
www.sadd.org

SADD is dedicated to preventing destructive decisions, specifically underage drinking, other drug use, impaired and risky driving, and teen violence and suicide. It has thousands of chapters in middle schools, high schools, and colleges.

Substance Abuse and Mental Health Services Administration (SAMHSA)
www.SAMHSA.gov

SAMHSA is responsible for overseeing and administering programs on mental health, drug abuse prevention, and drug treatment around the nation. For SAMHSA publications dealing with alcohol and other drug abuse, go to **www.store.samhsa.gov**.

The National PTA
www.pta.org

PTA works in cooperation with many national education, health, safety, and child advocacy groups and federal agencies to benefit children. The PTA website can help you locate a chapter, or offer information about organizing or running a PTA in your area.

White Bison Wellbriety Training Institute
www.whitebison.org

White Bison, Inc., Wellbriety Training Institute, is an American Indian nonprofit charitable organization that offers sobriety, recovery, addiction prevention, and wellness ("Wellbriety") learning resources to the Native American community nationwide.

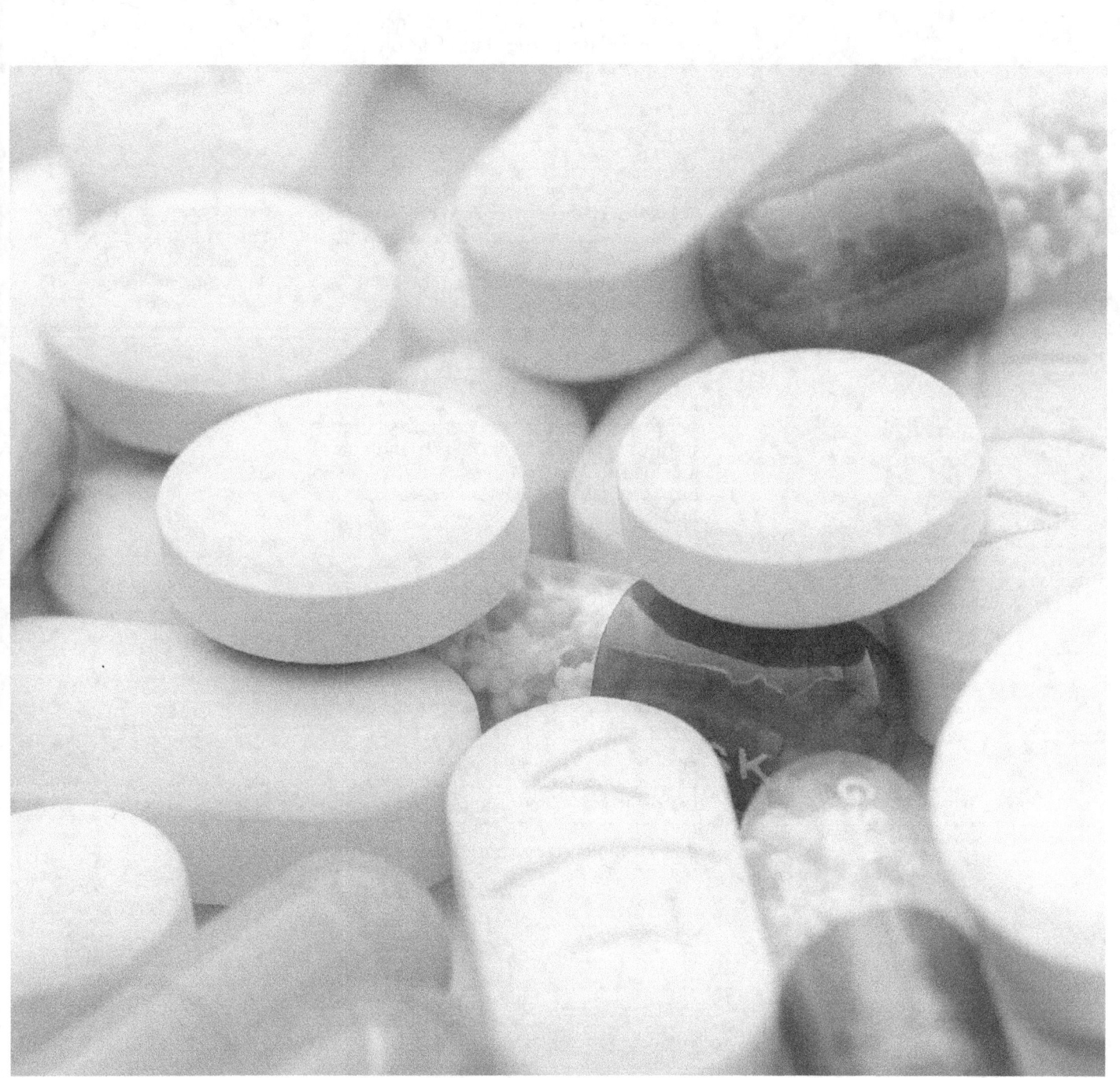

DRUG IDENTIFICATION CHART

	DRUG NAME(S)	OTHER NAME(S)

Prescription Medications – Narcotics (Opiods)

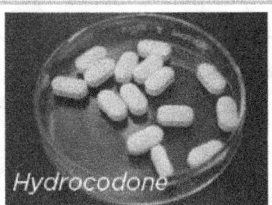
Hydrocodone

Hydrocodone is the most frequently prescribed opioid in the United States. Usually prescribed for pain or as a cough suppressant, it is the most abused opiod. The most prescribed brands are Vicodin, Lorcet, Lortab, Vicoprofen, and Hycomine.

Hydro, Norco, Vikes

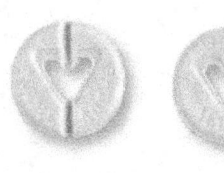
Oxycodone

Oxycodone products are very powerful painkillers. Examples include pharmaceutical drugs like OxyContin, Percodan, and Percocet.

Oxycotton, Percs, OC, OX, Oxy, Hillbilly Heroin, Kicker

Prescription Medications – Depressants – Barbiturates

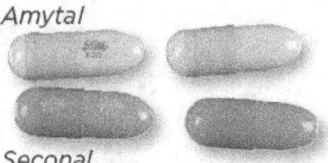
Amytal

Seconal

Amytal and Seconal are two barbiturates, which are depressants that slow down the central nervous system and cause sleepiness. Others include Fiorina, phenobarbital, Pentothal, and Nembutal.

Barbs, Block Busters, Christmas Trees, Goof Balls, Pinks, Red Devils, Reds & Blues, Yellow Jackets

Prescription Medications – Depressants – Benzodiazepines

Valium

Valium, Xanax, Halcion, Ativan, and Klonopin are the most common prescription benzodiazepines, which were developed to replace barbituates. Other brand names include ProSom, Dalmane, Restoril, Versed, Librium, Tranxene, Paxipam, Serax, Centrax, and Doral.

Benzos, Downers

Xanax

Prescription Medications – Stimulants

Ritalin

Adderall, Dexedrine, Concerta, Ritalin, Didrex, Bontril, Preludin, Fastin Adipex P, Ionomin, and Meridia are stimulants used to treat obesity, attention deficit and hyperactivity disorders (ADHD/ADD), and narcolepsy. Stimulants speed up the body's systems.

Ice, Crank, Speed, Bennies, Black Beauties, Uppers, Pellets, R-Ball, Skippy, Vitamin R, Illys

Anabolic Steroids

Android (Steroid)

Anabolic steroids are synthetically produced variants of the male hormone testosterone. When users stop taking steroids, they may experience severe depression and attempt suicide.

Arnolds, Juice, Pumpers, Roids, Stackers, Weight Gainers

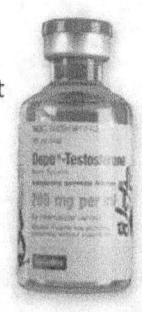
Testosterone

For more information about these and other drugs, visit **www.getsmartaboutdrugs.com**.

DESCRIPTION	HOW CONSUMED	MIND AND BODY EFFECTS	SEE PAGE(S)
Pill forms (including tablets and capsules), syrups.	Usually taken orally.	Euphoria, drowsiness, dizziness, nausea, constipation, urinary retention, and depressed respiration. Withdrawal symptoms include restlessness, muscle and bone pain, insomnia, diarrhea, and vomiting.	11
Pill forms (including tablets and capsules). *Percocet*	Usually taken orally.	Inability to concentrate, apathy, slowed physical activity, constricted pupils, flushing of the face and neck, constipation, nausea, vomiting, and slowed breathing. Withdrawal symptoms may include watery eyes, runny nose, yawning, sweating, restlessness, irritability, loss of appetite, nausea, tremors, severe depression, vomiting, increased heart rate and blood pressure, and alternating chills and sweating.	11
Pill forms (including tablets and capsules), syrups, and injectable liquids.	Swallowed (pill form) or injected (liquid form). Overdoses can occur easily and lead to death.	Mild euphoria, lack of inhibition, relief of anxiety and sleepiness, amnesia, reduced reaction time, impaired mental functioning and judgment, confusion, slurred speech, weakness, headache, lightheadedness, blurred vision, dizziness, nausea, vomiting, low blood pressure, and slowed breathing.	12
Pill forms (including tablets and capsules); Versed is available as an injectable liquid and as a syrup.	Usually taken orally (pill form) or crushed and snorted.	Sleepiness, amnesia, hostility, irritability, vivid or disturbing dreams, reduced reaction time, impaired mental functioning and judgment, confusion. May also cause slurred speech, loss of coordination, weakness, headache, lightheadedness, blurred vision, dizziness, nausea, vomiting, low blood pressure, and slowed breathing. Rarely fatal unless combined with other drugs or alcohol; withdrawal can be life threatening.	12
Pill forms (including tablets and capsules).	Usually taken orally but sometimes crushed and snorted or injected.	Increased activity, reduced appetite, wakefulness. Chronic use may cause agitation, hostility, panic, aggression, suicidal or homicidal tendencies, paranoia, and hallucinations. Large or extended doses may cause dizziness, tremors, headache, flushed skin, chest pain, excessive sweating, vomiting, and abdominal cramps.	12
Pill forms (including tablets and capsules), liquid drops, gels, creams, patches, injectable solutions.	Ingested orally, injected intramuscularly, or applied to the skin.	Dramatic mood swings, hostility, impaired judgment, and increased aggression (often called "roid rage"), high cholesterol levels and liver damage, viral infections (e.g., HIV/AIDS, hepatitis B or C), and bacterial infections. Males: early sexual development, acne, stunted growth, shrinking testicles, reduced sperm count, enlarged breast tissue, sterility, and increased risk of prostate cancer. Females: deep voice, increased facial and body hair, menstrual irregularities, male pattern baldness, and lengthening of the clitoris.	12-13

Street Drugs

Marijuana

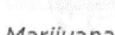

Marijuana is a mind-altering (psychoactive) drug produced by the Cannabis sativa plant. It contains over 400 chemicals; THC is believed to be the main chemical ingredient.

Marijuana cigarette, or "joint"

Aunt Mary, BC Bud, Blunts, Boom, Chronic, Dope, Gangster, Ganja, Grass, Hash, Herb, Hydro, Indo, Joint, Kif, Mary Jane, Mota, Pot, Reefer, Sinsemilla, Skunk, Smoke, Weed, Yerba

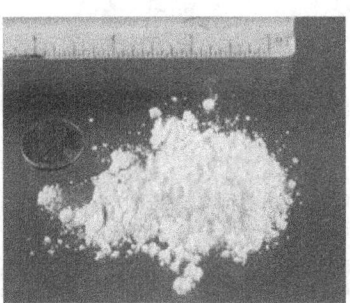

Cocaine

Cocaine is an intense, euphoria-producing stimulant drug with strong addictive potential. Very pure cocaine can cause cardiac arrhythmias, ischemic heart conditions, sudden cardiac arrest, convulsions, strokes, and death.

Coca, Coke, Crack, Flake, Snow, Soda Cot

Crack Cocaine

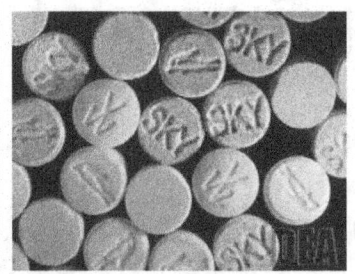

Ecstasy

Ecstasy tablets contain MDMA and other drugs that can be harmful; it is both a stimulant and psychedelic. In high doses, MDMA can interfere with the body's ability to regulate temperature, which can result in liver, kidney, and cardiovascular system failure—or death.

Adam, Beans, Clarity, Disco Biscuit, E, Ecstasy, Eve, Go, Hug Drug, Lover's Speed, MDMA, Peace, STP, X, XTC

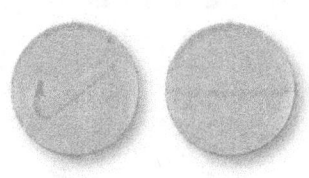

Methamphetamine

Methamphetamine (meth) is a highly addictive drug with potent central nervous system stimulant properties; the FDA-approved brand-name medication is Desoxyn. High doses may cause death from stroke, heart attack, or multiple organ problems caused by overheating.

Batu, Bikers Coffee, Black Beauties, Chalk, Chicken Feed, Crank, Crystal, Glass, Go-Fast, Hiropon, Ice, Meth, Methlies Quick, Poor Man's Cocaine, Shabu, Shards, Speed, Stove Top, Tina, Trash, Tweak, Uppers, Ventana, Vidrio, Yaba, Yellow Bam

Heroin

Heroin is a highly addictive drug and the most rapidly acting of the opiates. Because heroin abusers do not know the actual strength of the drug or its true contents, they are at a high risk of overdose or death.

Big H, Black Tar, Chiva, Hell Dust, Horse, Negra, Smack, Thunder

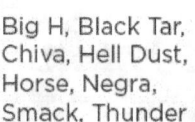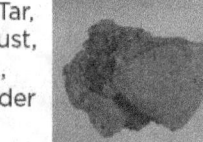

Black Tar Heroin

For more information about these and other drugs, visit **www.getsmartaboutdrugs.com**.

DESCRIPTION	HOW CONSUMED	MIND AND BODY EFFECTS	SEE PAGE(S)
Dry, shredded mix of flowers, stems, seeds, and leaves; typically green, brown.	Usually smoked as a cigarette (called a joint) or in a pipe or bong. Also smoked in blunts (cigars that have been emptied of tobacco and filled with marijuana), mixed with foods, or brewed as tea.	Bloodshot eyes, increased heart rate, coughing, increased appetite, decreased blood pressure, problems with memory and learning, distorted perception, difficulty thinking and solving problems, and loss of coordination. Long-term effects may include bronchitis, emphysema, and bronchial asthma; suppressed immune system; apathy; increased cancer risk; impaired judgment, memory, and concentration; loss of motivation, ambition, and interest. Withdrawal may cause headache, shakiness, sweating, stomach pains, nausea, restlessness, irritability, sleep difficulties, and decreased appetite.	13-14
Usually a white, crystalline powder. Cocaine base (crack) consists of small, irregularly shaped chunks (or "rocks") of a whitish solid.	Snorted or injected into the veins after dissolving in water (powder); smoked alone or with marijuana or tobacco (crack); used in combination with an opiate, like heroin, in a practice known as speedballing.	Euphoria, increased alertness and excitation, restlessness, irritability, increased blood pressure and heart rate, dilated pupils, insomnia, loss of appetite, and anxiety followed by mental and physical exhaustion, sleep, and depression. High doses or prolonged use can cause paranoia. Long-term inhaled use has led to a unique respiratory syndrome; chronic snorting of cocaine has led to the erosion of the upper nasal cavity.	16
Pill forms (including tablets and capsules) but also distributed in powder and liquid forms.	Usually by swallowing tablets, sometimes crushed and snorted, occasionally smoked (rarely injected). Also available as a powder. Commonly taken with other substances, such as alcohol and marijuana.	Increased motor activity, alertness, heart rate, and blood pressure; euphoria; increased sensitivity to touch, increased energy, and sensual and sexual arousal; unwanted effects include confusion, anxiety, depression, paranoia, sleep problems, muscle tension, tremors, involuntary teeth clenching, muscle cramps, nausea, faintness, chills, sweating, and blurred vision. May increase risk of long-term (perhaps permanent) problems with memory and learning.	14
Regular meth is a pill or powder; crystal meth resembles glass fragments or shiny blue-white "rocks" of various sizes. 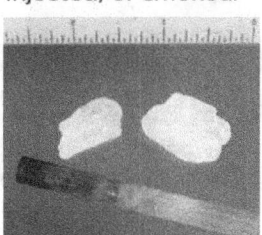	Swallowed, snorted, injected, or smoked.	Increased wakefulness, increased physical activity, decreased appetite, rapid breathing and heart rate, irregular heartbeat, increased blood pressure, extreme anorexia, memory loss, severe dental problems. Chronic abusers exhibit violent behavior, anxiety, confusion, insomnia, aggression, hallucinations, mood disturbances, delusions, and paranoia that can cause homicidal or suicidal thoughts.	14
Typically a white or brownish powder or a black sticky substance known on the streets as "black tar heroin."	Injected, smoked, or sniffed/snorted.	Euphoric surge (or "rush"), followed by wakefulness and drowsiness, respiratory depression, constricted pupils, nausea, warm flushing of the skin, dry mouth, and heavy extremities.	14

	DRUG NAME(S)	OTHER NAME(S)

Synthetic Drugs

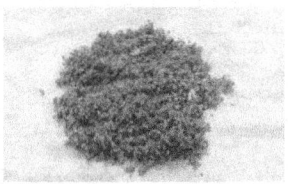

K2/Spice

K2/Spice is a mixture of herbs and spices, typically sprayed with a compound similar to THC, the psychoactive ingredients in marijuana. Often sold in drug paraphernalia stores ("head shops"), tobacco or retail stores, and online, it is often sold as incense or "fake weed."

Bliss, Black Mamba, Bombay Blue, Fake Weed, Genie, Spice, Zohai

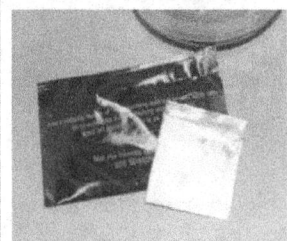

Bath Salts

"Bath salts" contain chemicals (synthetic stimulants) that are synthetic derivatives of cathinone, a central nervous system stimulant. Many of these products are sold over the Internet, in convenience stores, and in head shops.

Bliss, Blue Silk, Cloud Nine, Drone, Energy-1, Ivory Wave, Lunar Wave, Meow Meow, Ocean Burst, Pure Ivory, Purple Wave, Red Dove, Snow Leopard, Stardust, Vanilla Sky, White Dove, White Knight, White Lightening

Other

Inhalants

Inhalants are invisible, volatile substances in common household products. They produce chemical vapors that are inhaled to induce psychoactive or mind altering effects. Inhalants are often among the first drugs young children use. Signs of use include paint or stains on body or clothing, spots or sores around the mouth, red or runny eyes or nose, chemical breath odor.

Gluey, Huff, Rush, Whippets

Cold Medications

Dextromethorphan (DXM) is a cough suppressor found in more than 120 over-the-counter (OTC) cold medications. Abuse by teenagers and young adults is of particular concern. High doses combined with alcohol or other drugs may cause death.

CCC, Dex, DXM, Poor Man's PCP, Robo, Rojo, Skittles, Triple C, Velvet

Tobacco (photo by Sjschen)

Tobacco contains nicotine, one of the most highly addictive drugs used today. Teens who smoke cigarettes are much more likely to use marijuana than those who have never smoked.

Smoke, bone, butt, coffin nail, cancer stick

Alcohol

Alcohol is a drug that can interfere with brain development in adolescents and teens. Alcohol poisoning, which can happen the very first time someone drinks alcohol, can cause serious brain damage or death. Drinking at a young age also makes alcoholism more likely later in life.

Beer, wine, wine cooler, malt liquor, booze

For more information about these and other drugs, visit **www.getsmartaboutdrugs.com**.

DESCRIPTION	HOW CONSUMED	MIND AND BODY EFFECTS	SEE PAGE(S)
Typically small, silvery plastic bags of dried leaves and marketed as incense that can be smoked. May resemble potpourri.	Usually smoked in joints or pipes; also made into tea.	Short term affects include paranoia, panic attacks, and giddiness; increased heart rate and blood pressure. Long-term effects on humans are not fully known.	15
Fine white, off-white, or slightly yellow-colored powder; also tablets and capsules.	Usually ingested by sniffing or snorting but also taken orally, smoked, or put into a solution and injected into veins.	Agitation, insomnia, irritability, dizziness, depression, paranoia, delusions, suicidal thoughts, seizures, panic attacks, impaired perception of reality, reduced motor control, rapid heart rate (which may lead to heart attacks and strokes), chest pains, nosebleeds, sweating, nausea, vomiting, and decreased ability to think clearly.	15
Common household products such as glue, lighter fluid, cleaning fluids, and paint.	Breathed in through the nose or the mouth by sniffing, snorting, or bagging (inhaling fumes from substances sprayed or deposited inside a plastic or paper bag); huffing from an inhalant-soaked rag stuffed in the mouth; or inhaling from balloons filled with nitrous oxide.	Slurred speech, lack of coordination, euphoria, and dizziness, drowsiness, lingering headache, weight loss, muscle weakness, disorientation, inattentiveness, irritability, depression, unconsciousness, damage to the nervous system and other organs, sudden death.	9-11
Cough syrup, pill forms (including tablets and capsules), or powder.	Drinking liquid cough preparations or powder formulas (now sold over the Internet), or taking pills that are swallowed or crushed and put into drinks.	Mild stimulation, euphoria, hallucinations, confusion, inappropriate laughter, agitation, paranoia, hallucinations, sensory changes (e.g., feeling of floating), loss of coordination, over-excitability, lethargy, slurred speech, sweating, hypertension. DXM products often contain other ingredients that can cause liver damage, rapid heart rate, vomiting, seizures, and coma.	11
Dried, fermented leaves from the tobacco plant, usually brown.	Cigarettes, cigars, pipes, smokeless tobacco (chew, dip, snuff).	Addiction, heart and cardiovascular disease, cancer of the lung, larynx, esophagus, bladder, pancreas, kidney, and mouth; emphysema and chronic bronchitis; can cause spontaneous abortion, pre-term delivery, and low birth weight.	7-8
Liquids in various colors.	Orally.	Addiction (alcoholism), dizziness, slurred speech, disturbed sleep, nausea, vomiting, hangovers, impaired motor skills, violent behavior, impaired learning, fetal alcohol syndrome, respiratory depression, and, at high doses, death.	8-9